SUMMARY

Nigeria's continuation as a cohesive functioning state is important to the United States due to the bilateral economic relationship, Nigeria's influence in the international community, and its pivotal role for U.S. interests in Sub-Saharan Africa. Despite the importance of Nigeria to the United States, the centrifugal forces that tear at the country's unity and the centripetal forces which have kept Nigeria whole are not well understood and are rarely examined. Those who make or execute U.S. policy will find it difficult to advance U.S. interests in Africa without an understanding of the pressures that bind and tear Nigeria.

This monograph examines why Nigeria is important to the United States, and the historic, religious, cultural, political, physical, demographic, and economic factors that will determine if Nigeria remains whole. It identifies Nigeria's major fault lines and makes policy recommendations for the United States to support Nigerians in their efforts to maintain a functioning and integrated state and, by so doing, advance U.S. interests.

NIGERIAN UNITY: IN THE BALANCE

The existence of Nigeria as a unified state is in jeopardy. Nigeria's continuation as a cohesive functioning state is important to the United States due to the bilateral economic relationship, Nigeria's role in the international community, and its centrality to U.S. interests in Sub-Saharan Africa. Despite the importance of Nigeria to the United States, the centrifugal forces that tear at the country's unity and the centripetal forces that have kept Nigeria whole are not well understood and are rarely examined. Those who make or execute U.S. policy will find it difficult to advance U.S. interests without an understanding of the pressures that bind and tear Nigeria.

This monograph examines why Nigeria is important to the United States and the historical, religious, cultural, political, physical, demographic, and economic factors that will determine if Nigeria remains whole. It identifies Nigeria's major fault lines and makes policy recommendations for U.S. support to Nigerians in their efforts to maintain a functioning and integrated state and, by so doing, advance U.S. interests.

NIGERIA'S IMPORTANCE TO THE UNITED STATES

Nigeria is central to U.S. interests in Sub-Saharan Africa and important to U.S interests beyond the African continent. Its value to the United States is best understood in the context of post-Cold War Sub-Saharan Africa's growing strategic importance.[1] This is primarily due to Sub-Saharan Africa's expanding role

1

in supplying the world economy, including key U.S. allies and potential rivals, with oil, gas, and nonfuel minerals. This has been highlighted by the expansion of efforts of emerging powers to obtain greater access to Sub-Saharan African resources and markets with China, in particular, achieving notable success.[2]

In rough tandem with its global role, Sub-Saharan Africa's significance to the United States has grown as it supplies a steadily growing amount of oil to the United States, and its commercial market is also growing in significance as U.S. companies tap into non-extractive sectors of the Sub-Saharan economy. The United States has already become Sub-Saharan Africa's second-largest industrial supplier, with American businesses exporting over $6 billion worth of goods to Africa in 2010 and importing goods from Africa worth more than $16 billion.[3]

In this context, U.S. Government agencies have identified specific U.S. economic and related security objectives in Africa as preserving access to natural resources, deterring violent extremist activities (especially those linked to international terrorist organizations), and reducing maritime piracy and African-based international crime. In addition, ongoing American humanitarian interests in resolving destabilizing humanitarian crises, human rights abuses, and health crises with implications for global health are also often stressed in Africa.[4] These objectives should not be seen in isolation, but rather as interrelated ways to achieve a prosperous and stable Africa that, in turn, will help achieve the wider strategic U.S. goal of a benign environment for global security and growth.[5]

The centrality of the Federal Republic of Nigeria to the achievement of these interests is difficult to overstate. Nigeria is the single most important Sub-Saharan

African source of oil for the United States. It supplies 11 percent of U.S. oil imports, making it America's fourth-largest supplier in 2011.[6] Nigeria ranks 10th in the world in proven oil reserves with 37.2 billion barrels, 10th in production, and eighth in exports. With 5.292 trillion cubic meters of natural gas reserves, Nigeria rates eighth in the world. However, natural gas production and exports rank much lower, since this resource has not been adequately harnessed, but is anticipated to replace oil as Nigeria's leading foreign exchange earner.[7] Nigeria, by virtue of its central location, large population, diverse and dynamic economy, and huge oil reserves, is a major power in the region and one of the region's most politically and economically important states.[8] In fact, Nigeria's potential should make it the "great giant [that] . . . will assume the natural leadership" of Sub-Saharan Africa.[9]

Nigeria is also one of the few credible Sub-Saharan African security partners for the United States. Nigeria, which helped found the two principal organizations of African states—the African Union (AU) and the Economic Community of West African States (ECOWAS)—remains disposed and able to act regionally and, to some degree, outside the region. It has been a major contributor of military forces to security operations supported by the United States on the continent, notably in Liberia and Somalia. It has long been the largest African contributor to United Nations (UN) peacekeeping operations in Africa and beyond.[10] Nigerian leaders often state their ambitions to play a larger role on the international scene, and Nigeria was elected a member of the UN Security Council in 2011.

The United States, then, has both significant economic and security interests in Sub-Saharan Africa that depend upon Nigeria's continued constructive international role. Nigeria can play a productive role in the region and contribute to global economic growth as a large, economically powerful unified state. At best, no group of conceivable Nigerian successor states would have the resources to continue these positive roles. At worst, a collection of failed states would be sources of further spreading instability.

However, Nigeria's unity is threatened by disruptive forces that come from within its own borders. The most immediate threats to Nigeria's coherence, and therefore its ability to support U.S. interests while pursuing its own, are organized crime syndicates, which operate major crude oil theft operations, massive drug trafficking, numerous cybercrimes, and rampant piracy that affect U.S. (or allied) economic assets.[11] At the same time, regionally and ethnically based armed groups in Nigeria, some linked to international terrorist organizations, have attacked Nigerian targets and declared the United States to be their enemy.

Nigeria, then, is a key country that greatly affects U.S. interests in Africa. Nigeria is also a major source of environmental pollution in the region. Its large population routinely suffers from humanitarian and health crises. It is a source of criminal and extremist activities. It is also a major source of energy resources, a potentially large commercial market, and a stabilizing presence.

Nigeria's strategic location, large diverse population, diplomatic muscle, and growing economy will ensure that it plays an important role influencing U.S. and other global states' interests in Africa. For these reasons, U.S. policymakers need to better understand Nigeria and its people in order to best influence it to support mutual interests.

NIGERIA AS AN ENTITY

The fault lines along which Nigeria may devolve were established in the process of its very formation. Like most post-colonial African states, Nigeria is both a mosaic of tribes, related or allied ethnic or ideological groups, and nations now linked economically and politically under a common government in a colonially imposed territorial unit. The British colonial government created a unified Nigeria in 1914 to demarcate its area of control from those of its European competitors and because its northern protectorate was too poorly resourced to stand on its own. It was therefore created as a state by externally imposed fiat, not for any internal, organic reason. Before the British arrived, there was no shared national consciousness, culture, or language in Nigeria, nor was there any sentiment to coalesce its peoples into a coherent nation under colonial rule. After the formal amalgamation in 1914, a north–south split in the colonial administration remained as northern and southern Nigeria continued along divergent political, economic, and social development trends. The British then further divided the south into eastern and western political entities. In 1954, the British started Nigeria towards independence under a constitution that reinforced the three-region system with robust regional governments under a weak federal system. Thus at independence in 1960, Nigeria consisted politically of Western, Eastern, and Northern Regions, which effectively broke the south in two, while leaving the north intact.[12] These regions reinforced Nigeria's major geographical, cultural, and ethnic groupings with the Hausa and Fulani concentrated in the north, Yoruba in the southwest, and Igbo in the southeast. This configuration contin-

5

ued past independence until 1966 when the regions were abolished during the run up to the Biafran civil war.[13] The rough borders between these three areas may become Nigeria's major fault lines along which the country could divide.

The British had created a unifying constitution, in an attempt to preserve the integrity of Nigeria as single unit, but it was an inherently unstable state structure that failed to survive for even a short while. Modern Nigeria, more so than other post-colonial African states with similar arbitrary borders and conjoined peoples, emerged "from a colonial state that had never successfully integrated its different constituent parts — indeed that never intended to form a coherent 'nation' and a corresponding national consciousness."[14]

With varying success, subsequent post-independence governments repeatedly attempted structural reform to build a legal and constitutional framework to govern a united Nigeria. Since independence in 1960, Nigeria has endured three republics, numerous military dictatorships and unsuccessful coups, and both British parliamentary and American presidential forms of government, with none able to adequately deliver stability or a sense of unity to the country.[15] The creation of its governmental structure both unified the country as a political entity while incorporating fundamental political geographic divisions. Nigeria's subsequent political evolution has not balanced these built-in centripetal and centrifugal forces. To understand these tensions, it is necessary to examine the underlying religious, cultural, political, physical, demographic, and economic forces that hold Nigerians together as an entity and threaten the state with fragmentation.

CROSS AND CRESCENT

The most important political fault line, the one between the North and the South, is reinforced by their different religious orientations. In fact, the role of religious affiliations in Nigeria has become increasingly important, grown violent,[16] and demonstrates how proximity to past foreign pressures "continues to affect many aspects of Nigerian history and culture."[17] Although traditional religious beliefs were once as numerous and pervasive as the many ethnic groups with which they were affiliated, by some estimates, less than 10 percent of Nigerians today exclusively practice the animist beliefs of their ancestors.[18] Since their earliest contacts, Muslim and Christian missionaries have zealously converted indigenous Nigerians, so that approximately 50 percent of Nigerians today may be Muslim and 40 percent Christian—and both now compete directly against one another.[19]

Christianity was introduced in the eastern part of Nigeria during the 15th century by Portuguese traders.[20] Non-Catholic forms of Christianity spread under British influence from the coast during the 1800s to establish itself among the southeast, central, and partially in the southwest and northeast populations of Nigeria. With this new faith, some minority ethnic groups reasserted themselves against the acculturating dominance of Islamic rule to which northern minorities were subordinated, while others embraced the success imparted to the middle class and elites that Christian-Western values rewarded under British rule.[21]

Under the British governing system of indirect rule, however, Islamic institutions were protected where they already existed, which hobbled Christian missionary activity in these mainly northern areas.[22] There were exceptions, however, as with the Yoruba of the southwest, who split between the two major religions when many Ijebu tribesmen accepted Anglicanism and British rule after a military defeat in 1892, while others remained Muslim.[23] In the south, Yoruba elites tried to use Christianity to forge a unified Yoruba political and cultural identity.[24] This was partially successful among the Christian Yoruba, while introducing new strains between Christian and non-Christian Yoruba. As a side effect, stress on a common Christian identity increased ties with Christians in other ethnic groups. It also highlighted differences between the more Christian South and the North, where Islam had already provided a common identity.

Islam arrived with Arab travelers and scholars across the northern Saharan trade routes in the 9th century.[25] It was slowly adopted in the north and west by already reigning dynastic rulers who used Islam to legitimize their rule; promote internal unity; organize their administrations; and gain the commercial, intellectual, and military advantages of association with the greater Islamic community. The Sefawa dynasty of the Kanem-Borno Empire of northern Nigeria, for example, ruled for over 1,000 years, in large part because of the unity and practices conveyed by Islam. From the 1800s onward, the powerful Sokoto caliphate ruled smaller Islamic states in northern Nigeria. It not only enabled stability and prosperity, but also forced mass conversions to Islam when needed.[26] During the first half of the 19th century, this caliphate became the largest system of theoretical political allegiance in Sub-Saharan Africa. It never functioned as a centralized government, however, nor was it imposed primarily by conquest. It represented a connected series of *coup d'états* by Muslim and Fulani elements whose leaders were awarded the title of emirs, but were, in effect, independent rulers. The Fulani emirs sought to establish better standards of Islamic observance and banded together in case of outside attack, but otherwise did not interfere in local governance. The minor states annexed into larger formations retained their identity, even as a common Islamic culture took hold.[27] Gradually, Islam became "the common culture that transcended ethnicity . . ." in the north, and Islamic Sharia law applied "more widely, and in some respects more rigidly . . . than anywhere else outside of Saudi Arabia."[28]

Traditionally, Nigerian Muslims are predominantly Sunni of the Qadiriyya orders within the Sufi movement, the more mystical form of Islam, organized in related, but independent, lodges. However, the competing Tijaniyya order was embraced by some Nigerians to counter the entrenched Qadiriyya structure, which resulted in frequent clashes over economic and political power between the two Sufi orders during much of the 20th century.[29] Both, in turn, were challenged by the Izala movement. Founded during the 1970s in the city of Jos (a city marked by violent clashes between immigrating ethnic groups), it vehemently opposed the mysticism of Sufism in favor of a more "orthodox" and public role for Islam. Izala has particularly attracted young men hoping to change old political and religious structures, but this burgeoning youthful population is also increasingly attracted to more militant armed groups, including *Kala-Kato*, *yan Bori*, and Iranian-connected groups.[30]

Although overt Muslim missionary work by Nigerians had traditionally been directed primarily toward animists and "backsliding" Muslims, this changed in recent times, most markedly in the 1980s. Partially inspired by foreign Muslim missionaries, some Nigerian Muslims began to direct their efforts towards Christians, with often violent rhetoric.[31] The most destabilizing of such Muslim groups may be *Jama'atu Ahlis Sunna Lidda'awati Wal-Jihad* or Boko Haram, as it is popularly known, formed in northern Nigeria's Borno state in 2002. It has announced plans to tie itself more closely to al-Qaeda in the Islamic Maghreb and to the Shabab, al-Qaeda's ally in Somalia. Recent American intelligence assessments have reportedly found that Boko Haram has trained with al-Qaeda-linked militants in camps in the deserts of Mali and may seek to expand its campaign of violence beyond Nigeria.[32] The U.S. Department of State designated three of its key leaders as Specially Designated Global Terrorists in June 2012.[33] Sometimes also called the Nigerian Taliban, it calls for strict observance of Sharia law throughout Nigeria, not just the 12 predominately Muslim states of the north where it is now used for Muslims (although only two states have applied it rigorously).[34]

There is no national or regional organization that can exercise religious authority over Islam or Christianity in Nigeria. Both religions have shown a strong tendency to divide into sub-sects, often strongly opposed to co-religionists. In addition, both have grown in part from politically inspired conversions. Under increased economic and social pressure, this tendency to divide into ever more fragmented and divisive sub-sects with political intentions has notably increased in modern times. Overt struggles between the major groups break out as well. Southeast states, like Cross River, resist the northern states' move to Sharia law by implementing "Christian Law" as a counter.[35] Religious competition is often politicized, which compounds the many ethnic and regional differences.

Although these religious, ethnic, cultural and regional affiliations are often exploited as the basis for discord in Nigeria, they do not necessarily condemn Nigeria to factionalization. The Yoruba serve as a modern example of coexistence, since many Muslim, Christian, and animist Yoruba dwell peacefully, not only in the same cities, but also in the same households.[36] Even some northern Christians have accepted Sharia law as a better way to protect their lives and property than the current corrupt system.[37] Historically, Nigerians have shown they can tolerate one another and thrive despite their differences. Conflicts are generally exceptions that must be managed. They are not indicative of inevitable and intractable conflicts in greater Nigerian society.[38]

THE CULTURES AND REGIONS

With a very large population packed into a relatively small but diverse physical region, a remarkable number of distinct groups have emerged from which Nigerians may draw strength through diversity or fracture along acrimonious cultural and regional lines. Depending on the characteristics used to distinguish its peoples—including language history, ancestral affiliation, food, customs, social organization, housing, settlement pattern, and location—there exist between 200 and 350 different ethnic groups in Nigeria.[39] Ten groups comprise 80 percent of the population, with four language groups—Hausa (21 percent), Yoruba (20), Igbo (17), and Fulani (7)—dominating.[40] The Igbo, Yoruba, and Hausa (the Hausa and Fulani are usually considered as allied groups in Nigeria) may be considered as ethnicities or "nationalities" knitted out of smaller sub-units that do not necessarily have a traceable blood relationship, but are united by a common culture and language. The Ilesha, Egba, Itshekiri Ijaw, and some other peoples of Nigeria, however, may be described as distinct tribes.[41]

Each ethnic group is associated with an ancestral homeland with the Hausa and Fulani in the north, Yoruba in the southwest, and Igbo in the southeast. This means the north is most influenced by Muslim Arab traditions and the south by Western British customs. The rough divisions between these three areas may be considered Nigeria's major political seams, as they divide Nigeria geographically, culturally, and ethnically. However, there are few ethnically "pure" areas. The intermixture and interspersing of ethnic groups has been a common historical occurrence in Nigeria, with 60 ethnic groups living in the small Niger Delta, for example, and the northeast area containing nearly half of Nigeria's ethnic groups.[42] Rapid urbanization has also attracted migrants from throughout the country so that nearly every ethnic group can be found intermingled in major cities like Kano and Lagos.[43]

The cultural traits of ethnic groups vary greatly. The Yoruba are traditionally more urbanized with a highly organized social structure. The Igbo are traditionally organized no higher than the clan level; they stress individual achievement and personal advancement, and value education highly. The Igbo are often "resented by other ethnic groups for their competitiveness and for their success."[44] Cultural differences such as these may irritate ethnic relations, especially where there is a large successful immigrant minority, which accounts for some of the backlash against the Igbo that precipitated both the Nigerian civil war and more recent violence.

Before British colonialism, Nigerians' cultural and regional differences could be seen as a source of interdependence, and "each community had specific attributes for which it was known, a specific contribution that it made for the overall well-being of the entire region."[45] Prominent Nigerian historian Adiele Afigbo noted in southeastern Nigeria that different cultures sought ties with each other to leverage their strengths, causing so much cultural overlap "that it was impossible to tell geographically where one group of people ended and another began."[46] Widespread contact fostered interethnic marriages, occupation-based secret societies, cultural exchanges, and complimentary economic relationships that allowed, for instance, largely conflict-free relations between the Yoruba and Hausa throughout the 20th century, except for two rare instances settled by mediation.[47]

In many ways, British rule continued the historic trend toward Nigerian "coherence"[48] by the imposition of English as Nigeria's official and most common second language; English common law along with Islamic and traditional laws; and a more modern economic structure and education system.[49] These changes also unified Nigerians in an unintended way by creating an educated elite at British schools. This elite used English to bridge ethnic divides in order to ameliorate the effects of colonialism and eventually overthrow it. To protest British rule, these elite members encouraged nationalism as "expressed in cultural ways, that is, in deliberate efforts to promote Nigerian food, names, forms of dress, languages, and even religions."[50] However, the political consciousness that might have enhanced a sense of Nigerian nationality and united the disparate ethnic groups within the borders of the former colony, also took the form of ethnic nationalism, emphasizing local ethnic culture and traditions. Nationalists succeeded in wresting independence from the foreign colonialists but failed to integrate the country into a whole.

As they competed for power, prestige, and associated benefits, nationalist elites sought support from members of their own ethnic groups by stressing ethnic differences. Drawing on the British policy of indirect rule, which endorsed or created local leaders (but not necessarily inheritable national institutions), different cultural and ethnic groups were mobilized for objectives that ostensibly ranged from regional autonomy to the total breakup of Nigeria. Their formation of political parties along ethnic and regional lines during the colonial period created an aggressive regionalism based on cultural, religious, and economic differences.[51] For example, the Northern People's Congress (NPC) was formed by northern educated elites in 1949, while the National Council for Nigeria and the Cameroons (NCNC) started as a national political party, but was quickly taken over by Igbo political leaders. In the west, the *Egbe Omo Oduduwa* metamorphosed into a political party, the Action Group, dominated by Yorubas in 1951. These regional political parties sought to advance regional and ethnic interests. They did so partially by defining other ethnic groups as political rivals.

Although successful in unifying enduring bases of local support, this process took ethnic hostility to a new level.[52] The development of creating and exacerbating friction between the different ethnic groups as part of a deliberate political strategy was a major factor in the disastrous Igbo attempt to secede in the 1967 Biafra War. In fact, membership in political parties was primarily determined by ethnicity until the 1990s, when ideology and platforms became more important. Increased Nigerian nationalism, spurred by urbanization, increasing pride in national symbols, and the horrors of the Biafra War, all weakened sectionalism in political life.[53]

MANY PEOPLES, MANY SYSTEMS

Although sectionalism was weakened by the emerging national political process, it did not disappear — partially because of the different political experiences of the various ethnic groups in Nigeria. Pre-colonial Nigeria's many societies governed themselves through a variety of political structures with differing economic bases. In the north, the Hausa and Fulani developed Muslim-based emirates and the caliphate, while the southwest had centralized Yoruba and Benin Kingdoms. In the southeast, the geography and diffuse settlement patterns supported less centralized, more democratic village-based hierarchies. Throughout pre-colonial Nigeria, additional small independent societies resided among these other entities.[54] Although these societies were mainly autonomous, they maintained "sophisticated interrelationships" that recognized commonalities and linkages among them.[55] British rule of Nigeria through its policy of indirect rule, or Native Authority, tried to use these pre-existing traditions and structures as the British understood them, but was ultimately unsuccessful in maintaining cultures or inter-Nigerian relationships.[56]

Strong British influence in Nigeria began in the early 1800s as interdiction efforts against the trans-Atlantic slave trade. By the 1860s, the British had established themselves in Lagos to better fight slavery and develop more legitimate trade. In 1898, the British converted lands previously granted to the private Royal Niger Company (RNC) in the north, creating the Protectorate of Northern Nigeria, which was united with the southern protectorate in 1914 to form a unified territory.[57]

The British governed the new union through a policy of indirect rule "to protect and empower traditional social structures, thereby making the colonial experience as unobtrusive as possible"[58] to local inhabitants by using the "institutions they themselves had invented."[59] This method was formed and used most successfully in the north where established authorities served as proxies for the British. However, it came at the expense of societal growth. The north was especially hampered in adopting Western education, which in turn retarded economic growth compared to the south.[60] Nonetheless, the British controlled "uncivilized or inappropriate" behavior such as the harsher measures in Islamic law.[61]

Indigenous rule and indirect rule did not coordinate well in the south. This forced traditional cultures to change, imposed alien governing schemes, and implemented policies that were a "disaster." Proof of these failures were seen in the subsequent riots in the southwestern city of Abeokuta in 1918 and Aba in the southeast in 1929.[62] Inevitably, colonial governance changed societies throughout Nigeria, twisting indigenous structures and relations until they were ineffective, but not replacing them sufficiently with Western substitutes.[63] Thus began the problems that continue into today, including competing sectional and sectarian interests and the tendency of political leaders to exploit ethnic and religious rivalries rather than build national interests and unity.[64]

Subdividing a state composed of ethnic groups in conflict is often used as a way to spread power and alleviate minorities' fears of stronger groups. However, in the case of Nigeria, it enabled regionalism and political conflict by entrenching the political parties of the three major ethnic groups.[65] Independent Nigeria continued this practice when the Midwestern Region was carved from the Western Region during a violent crisis in 1963.[66] After Nigeria's first military coup in 1966, General Johnson Aguiyi-Ironsi feared the creeping fragmentation of Nigeria along cultural fault lines. He abolished the regions and the accompanying preferential treatment given to indigenous groups in their homeland. Rioting began in the north, and a counter-coup set in motion the violent ethnic conflicts that initiated the attempted secession of the Eastern Region to become Biafra and Nigeria's bloody civil war.[67]

The new leader, General Yakubu Gowan, declared an emergency and divided the country into 12 states[68] to allay fears of domination by any one group and to reduce the strength of the oil producing Eastern Region.[69] Once the Biafran secession was crushed in 1970, splintering continued with the number of federal states increasing to 19 in 1976, 21 in 1987, 30 in 1991, and 36 in 1996.[70] Although more minority groups are appeased by having greater influence within one of the 36 states, not all of the over 250 ethnic groups were satisfied since most do not have their own homeland by which to control revenues from the central government.[71] The major ethnic groups are also unhappy since their influence is diluted — with the former Northern Region, for example, now fractured into 19 states. Whether the existence of these many states will act as the balancer against domination by major ethnic groups remains to be seen.[72] However, a call for 35 more states was made in 1994, although the current number seems firm in the 1999 constitution that established the fourth republic.[73]

Creating new states attempts to address the problems of ethnic and religious balance, but fracturing creates smaller and weaker states, some of which are not economically viable without the support of shared federal revenues. Many small states also increase the relative power of the central government with respect to the states and may have been intentionally created to remove future threats of secession.[74]

This fragmented arrangement has also proven so politically unwieldy that an informal arrangement of six geopolitical zones[75] was developed for power sharing among the regional elites, with each of the top federal positions to be rotated among one representative from each zone.[76] Although a balancing mechanism, zoning hardly fosters unity, as each top official may not be selected on merit and may represent his zone's interests over that of the country.[77] This system was already out of kilter by the election of southern President Goodluck Jonathan in 2011, when many Northerners felt that this cycle was theirs to fill the presidency.[78] The regionalization, fracturing, and zoning of Nigeria have not stabilized the competing demands of ethnic, religious, economic, and political constituents.

From historic political structures to partisan modern party activities, politics has been a mostly divisive force in Nigeria, with strong communal tendencies overbearing statewide interests. Colonial governing seemed to have reinforced detrimental elements of local governing systems without reinforcing positive aspects or establishing a better workable arrangement. Modern Nigerians have resorted to factionalizing their state to accommodate ethnic fears and aspirations through a method that seems to have established an unwieldy governing system that reinforces fragmentation of the state.

THE LAND

Without a well-rooted national, political, or ideological identity, Nigeria can then be seen less as a single nation-state and more as a complex region resulting from many interacting influences and conflicting pressures over its long rich history. The most basic of these influences, the nature of the physical environment itself, has both unified and divided Nigeria. Aspects of Nigeria's physical environment exercise centripetal influences, creating a natural unity for the country.[79] The widely diverse distribution of natural resources, such as the North's tin, iron ore, coal, limestone, lead, and zinc, and the South's crude oil and natural gas,[80] and resulting dissimilar economic opportunities led to a robust and complementary economy. This helped knit Nigeria together since the time of independence.

Nigeria's physical geography also unifies the country through its river systems and the potential for the regions to complement one another through human activities that harness local natural specialties. The Niger River and its main tributary, the Benue, unify Nigeria through major waterways and water sheds that define the country as a physical region distinct from its neighbors. Historically, these waterways are the primary lines of communication and commerce binding Nigerians together. Even here, however, rapids and falls common to the river systems, and large seasonal swings in water flow due to the monsoons, curtail navigation along some parts of the rivers.[81] The "Y" shape formed by the confluence of the Niger and Benue Rivers also creates and links three separate regions. Ironically, the very communication links between them are sometimes cited as dividing lines by Nigerians.

Nigeria's vast and diverse land area, about twice the size of California or four times that of the United Kingdom (UK), can be divided into two physical zones: the forest zone of the south with tropical forests and tall grass-derived savannah, and the grassland zone of the north with natural savanna and near desert condition sub-zones.[82] These geographic zones include seven relief zones that, along with proximity to the Gulf of Guinea, result in multiple climates ranging from humid tropical of the south to the arid semi-desert in the north.[83] Rainfall defines two distinct seasons, wet and dry, the length and intensity of each depending on the seasonal dominance of monsoonal dry winds from the Sahara and rain-giving winds from the Gulf of Guinea.[84] Thus the north may receive only 20 inches of rain during its 5-month rainy season, while the south may receive 120 inches over 9 months.[85]

Such physical differences result in varying types of vegetation. These differences in vegetation mean differences in the availability of agricultural pursuits, indigenous building materials, and types of settlement patterns[86] that shaped local cultures in different ways. The northern Sahel savanna and semi-desert allowed the formation of cattle raising, cavalry, and caravan based centralized states, with strong cultural influences from North Africa flowing along well-established trade and communication lines. The often impenetrable forests of the south protected the independence of small agriculture-based states and larger more egalitarian confederations. The even more difficult terrain of the southwest gave rise to the multiple tightly knit independent communities with separate languages that remained highly resistant to outside penetration or control. The physical environment allowed or encouraged the formation of communities with fundamentally different ways of life over which a political superstructure was imposed.

Physical geography, then, has helped shape and define cultural differences in Nigeria through variation in climate, vegetation and agricultural pursuits, availability of mineral resources, and the need to sustain the environment. Over 33 percent of Nigeria's land is arable (compared to 18 percent for the United States and 23 percent for the UK).[87] Throughout their history, agriculture has been Nigerians' main economic activity, still accounting for 30 percent of gross domestic product (GDP) and 70 percent of the labor force in 2010.[88] Water and land resources are thus critical to social stability throughout Nigeria. Guinea corn and palm are the main indigenous food crops in Nigeria, but maize, cassava, yams, rice, and some fruits have been successfully introduced over the past 2 centuries.[89] These are grown mainly for consumption in Nigeria and much of it by subsistence farmers who account for 60 percent of the working population.[90] Cotton, cocoa, peanuts, rubber, and palm oil are Nigeria's main commercial crops.

Climate and soil dictate where crops are grown, with more dry-tolerant crops like peanuts, grains, and cotton planted in the north; cocoa in the southwest; and palm, roots and tubers, and maize throughout the south.[91] In the north, the raising of livestock is a traditional agricultural pursuit adapted to the ever drier environment.[92] In the southwest, monsoonal conditions create a beneficial second short dry season that allows harvesting of two crops annually to better support an urban culture, while the transitional climate of the Middle Belt allows a wide variety of crops like tomatoes, yams, and soybeans.[93] Fishing is an important source for food and trade along the coast, in the Niger Delta, and in the north around Lake Chad, although the latter is diminishing due to reduction of the lake.[94] Commercial crops have also suffered, with cocoa production, the only remaining major agricultural export, dropping from 300,000 tons to 180,000 tons in 25 years.[95]

The dry north is particularly sensitive to changes in climate, and, since droughts in the 1970s and 1980s, the resulting shifts in human and animal patterns. For instance, demand for irrigation water among the four countries that border Lake Chad has quadrupled—much from demand in Nigeria—accounting for half of the 90 percent loss of surface area this once major body of water held in 1960.[96] The overall pressure of a rapidly growing population on land resources also contributes to over cropping, over grazing, and deforestation, resulting in soil impoverishment, erosion, and desertification in the north where the Sahara Desert advances by two to three miles every year.[97] The natural environment of Nigeria is degrading rapidly, pressuring its people, economy, and politics. In addition to an increase in overall stress, one immediate effect of environmental change has been increased internal migration with the consequent accentuation of existing fault lines or the creation of new ones.

A clear example of the differences can be seen in central Plateau State, which is located in the heart of the divide between the mercantile, largely Muslim pastoralist peoples of the north and the traditionally farming, mostly Christian peoples of the south. Here the mass movement of "Northern" herders into farming areas has accentuated existing fault lines between different cultures and ethnic groups. Agriculture and pastoralism have coexisted side-by-side for centuries, and many herding and farming communities in the same area have often developed usually beneficial interdependent relationships. However, in the last few decades, small-scale conflicts between herders and farmers have been repeatedly linked with other ethnic, political, and religious conflicts and escalated into widespread violence and displacement of people.

> For example, in 2004, President Obasanjo of Nigeria declared a state of emergency in Plateau State, when herder-farmer conflicts resulted in 'near-mutual genocide' of Christians and Muslims and more than 20,000 refugees fleeing to neighboring Cameroon . . .[98]

The flow of refugees into Jos, its largest city, combined with outside Muslim and Christian support (both Nigerian and foreign) for co-religionists, have greatly increased tension. Armed groups such as Boko Haram have used the opportunity to stage attacks and bombings on civilian targets in an apparent effort to expand the conflict, with the Nigerian government caught in the middle.

POPULATION

Shaped by Nigeria's physical geography, environmental pressures, and economic changes, the settlement and demographics of the population are marked by a pattern of uneven distribution. Nigeria's total population of 155,215,000 people as of 2011 makes it by far the most populous state in Africa and the 8th largest in the world. Its high birth rate of 1.9 percent (an average of 4.74 children born to a woman during her lifetime) means that Nigerian society currently counts 41 percent of its population below the age of 15, and its burgeoning population will double in size in just over 37 years at its present growth rate. Such numbers strain economic growth and human development, which is demonstrated through related poor health statistics: a life expectancy of 47.6 years in 2011 (220th in the world), 91.5 infant deaths out of 1,000 in their first year of life, and 840 maternal deaths out of 100,000 births, ranking respectively 10th and 9th worst in the world. A high risk of HIV/AIDS, malaria, and other tropical disease exposure in Nigeria explain, in part, these abysmal numbers.[99]

Nigeria has three main population clusters: the north around the city of Kano with a density of over 100 people per square mile, the southwest with a density of over 140, and the southeast with over 150.[100] In 2010, Nigeria's population was split evenly between urban and rural locations, but it is rapidly urbanizing at an annual rate of 3.5 percent.[101] In 1970, less than 10 percent of the population lived in towns of 50,000 people or more. Most of those were in the southwest where city living is part of traditional Yoruba culture, making them the most urbanized group in Africa.[102] In contrast, the Ibibio and Igbo people of the southeast live in a densely populated region, but traditionally dwelled in dispersed compounds or villages, not towns, due to the inability of the terrain and vegetation to support larger concentrated settlements.[103]

Rural to urban migration is the single most important movement of people in Nigeria. Since the 1970s, spells of drought in the Sahel have driven environmental refugees from northern Nigeria and neighboring countries into urban slums. Kano's population has increased by 14 fold in just 45 years, to 3.6 million, making it the second largest city in Nigeria.[104] Refugees from politics and violence also drive migration in Nigeria. There have been movements after many recent ethnic clashes, including one million Nigerians displaced between 1999 and 2004[105] and the Nigerian Civil War's 1.8 million refugees from 1967 to 1970. Movement goes as far back as the early 1800s when thousands founded wartime refugee camps that became the modern Yoruba cities of Abeokuta, Oke-Odan, Ibadan, and Ijaye.[106] Economic opportunity is a third reason for internal migration, as showcased by people of southeast Nigeria whose poor agricultural land, high unemployment, and few local opportunities "forced many of the people, most especially the Igbo, to immigrate to other Nigerian cities as traders."[107] The success of the Igbo as small business men and civil servants often make their presence as migrants in other parts of Nigeria resented by indigenous people.[108]

The southwest coastal city of Lagos is the epitome of these trends. Its population of 10.2 million makes it one of the world's 25 megacities.[109] Encountering grinding poverty and lacking the support and restraints of their ethnic cultures, many urban migrants have not successfully integrated into their new environs, making this predominately youthful population "prone to lawlessness and violence" and creating intercommunal clashes.[110] Thus a combination of factors makes for uneasy tensions between migrant and local populations.

One demographic indicator of particular interest is education, for the divisions it represents and the unity it offers. Education is often embraced as the means to reverse undesired economic and developmental trends for the betterment of society. However, only about two-thirds of the Nigerian population is literate, averaging 9 years of schooling. The difference between male and female literacy is about 15 percent, with a 2-year spread in education.[111] Unfortunate as those numbers are, the regional and cultural differences in embracing Western-style education bode worse for Nigerian unity and progress.

Southern Nigeria readily adopted western education, and the Christianity that went hand-in-hand with it, during the colonial period.[112]

> Through this, the Southern elite was . . . able to dominate the civil service and other sectors that demanded formal educational training. . . . Formal education also proved an advantage in raising loans from the banks, providing funds to start or consolidate new businesses.[113]

Western-style education grew faster in the south than in the north,[114] where well-established Islamic societies favored their own religious based education systems and, often with good reason, suspected a Christian agenda even in allegedly secular Western education. These suspicions persist. It is telling that the name of Boko Haram, the Nigerian Islamic terrorist group, means "Western education is sinful" (forbidden by Islamic law); and the group repeatedly attacks schools.[115] The violence against Igbos at the opening of the Nigerian civil war was due in part to Northerners, reaction against a unitary federal government, which "aroused fears in the north that the more highly educated Igbos would soon dominate the federal government."[116]

Thus literacy rates, school enrollment, and success in national examinations decrease the further north each is measured, and "female literacy is as low as 21 percent in the northeast and north."[117] Islamic schools have not resolved the education gap. In Kano state in

2010 for instance, 80 percent of the 3.7 million of those between 5 and 21 years of age are estimated to attend some form of Islamic school, either exclusively or in addition to a state school. "Many of these neither live up to parents' moral expectations nor impart the skills necessary for developing the region."[118]

Western-style education remains an important means for modern advancement, however, and was a crucial element shared by the elite that deposed British imperialism and established Nigeria's modern sovereignty. Common experience in Western-style schools "enabled the elite to come together, thus overcoming some of the barriers created by ethnic and regional divisions."[119] Education became both a unifying factor (providing common ground for those, especially the elites, who received it) and a centrifugal factor, particularly in pre-independence days, for those who saw it as a Christianizing agent[120] or as yet another institution dominated by the South.[121]

Recognizing education's divisive and unifying potential, Nigerian nationalists used a mass educational program to reform colonial society and address the regional educational imbalance to foster national integration in the 1960s. U.S. assistance through the Carnegie Corporation, motivated partly by Cold War politics during the era of decolonization, played a significant role in reforming the elitist British educational system. This made it possible for Nigerians to link the opening to education for different classes and the expansion of access across regional lines to the larger project of economic development and nation building.[122] Most importantly, this effort helped create and spread a common English-speaking national Nigerian culture.

The demographics of the Nigerian people hold promise as a unifying factor through education and integrated settling, while also posing pressures through poorly addressed health needs, rapid population growth, poorly managed urbanization, as well as suspicion of Western education by some and inadequate literacy for modernization.

THE ECONOMY

Perhaps the greatest single factor shaping the Nigerian economy is the change from a relatively integrated agricultural-based economic system with a growing manufacturing based sector to a highly concentrated single resource-based economy. In pre-colonial days, commercial routes united Nigerians who traded coastal fish and salt for kola nuts and cassava from the forests; beans, horses, and cattle products from the north; and yams from the Middle Belt.[123] Although much of Nigeria's food today is imported, the age-old trade in regionally raised food stuffs continues between north and south, reinforcing their co-dependency.[124] Beyond the roads, river transportation networks bind the country, as noted earlier, as do the railroads built by the British in the late 1800s and early 1900s. The railroads improved inter-Nigerian trade in food and cash crops, exported minerals from the interior, allowed the spread of ideas, and fostered migration to pursue economic opportunities — thus more closely integrating northern and southern Nigeria.[125] Nigeria's economic differences make its regions depend upon and complement one another.

PETROLEUM POLITICS

At independence in 1960, the economy was then relatively well-integrated. Agriculture was the mainstay of the economy as well as the cultural base of most ethnic groups. In 1964, it contributed 61 percent of the GDP and 71 percent of total exports. Nigeria was not only self-sufficient in food production, but also was an exporter until 1973.

Economic integration began to unravel as oil rose to dominate the Nigerian economy. Since its discovery in 1956, oil has played an ever greater and now all-consuming role in Nigeria's economy, politics, and society.[126] Petroleum's share of GDP rose from 1 percent in 1960 to 26 percent in 1970, and its share of total export revenue grew to 94 percent by 1976.[127] As investment shifted, agriculture's contribution to GDP and total exports quickly fell.[128] Further undercutting local producers, crude oil earnings were primarily used for huge imports of consumables.[129] This transformed the material base of society.[130] High government revenue derived from easily controllable petroleum created a classic "rentier" state, with the government receiving revenue streams independent of broadly based taxation and the electorate, and hence largely unaccountable to its people.

A similar crowding out of investment was seen in the once promising manufacturing sector. Pre-colonial Nigeria had a long tradition of industry that exploited available natural resources like cotton for textiles and palm for oil processing and soap production.[131] During the colonial period, Western economic influence, especially a monetary base for the economy, rooted quickly and deeply among the coastal societies, but was resisted in the more static cultures of the north, economically widening the existing physical, cultural, and religious gaps.[132] These were the foundations for larger scale manufacturing starting in the 1950s.[133] Over the last 2 decades, manufacturing based on Nigeria's natural resources continued with the production of petroleum-derived chemicals and fertilizers, paper and pulp, steel, cement, textiles, beverages, food stuffs, and rubber products.[134] Most of these industries are located in vibrant southern Nigeria where natural resources, capital, and a better educated work force are centered.[135] But manufacturing remains starved of investment and infrastructure, which is more often geared towards extraction activities. In electrical generation, for example, Nigeria produces only 40 percent of the country's needs, forcing manufacturers and households to resort to expensive electrical generators for power.[136] With a heavy focus on oil production, a long tradition of manufacturing in Nigeria has been unable to progress sufficiently due in large part to poor policies, lack of investment, and insufficient infrastructure.

Nigeria's economy is large, reflecting its huge population and centuries of integration into the global economy. The Nigerian economy ranks 32nd in the world in GDP purchasing power parity, with $378 billion in 2010, and a very healthy real growth rate averaging over 7 percent since 2003.[137] However, a dismal economic record for the decades preceding this recent spurt dropped per capita income from a promising $1,500 during the 1970s to less than $300 in 1998 before recovering to $1,470 per capita GDP (official exchange rate) in 2010.[138] During the worst period (1980-2000), Nigeria's poverty rate doubled to 70 percent where it stubbornly remained until 2007 (the latest figures available). Even the recent higher growth rates can create ethnic friction when development opportunities bring together previously separated groups, with new arrivals resented by the natives.[139] Nigeria's great economic potential has so far been under-realized, with a "scarcity of economic activities foster[ing] competition over resources."[140]

CORRUPTION

The most harmful effect of the vast sums petroleum brings to Nigeria is almost certainly the equally vast corruption it leaves in its wake. Widespread corruption explains much of the poor performance in all of Nigeria's economic sectors. Transparency International, the corruption nongovernment organization (NGO) watchdog, rated the perception of corruption in Nigeria's public sector at 2.4 (where 10 is the cleanest government). This places Nigeria at 143 of 180 countries measured.[141] Corruption has dogged the government for decades, with up to a quarter of oil revenues "disappeared," and Nigeria's anti-corruption chief reporting "70% of Nigeria's oil wealth was wasted or stolen in 2003, however, by 2005 the number dipped to 'only' 40%."[142] The scale of corruption has grown alongside the revenues collected from oil, giving the ruling elite easy access to state money and shorting its citizens of economic and human development funds.[143]

Deepening poverty throughout the country is widely blamed on Nigeria's leaders who are often seen as "only looking after their own interests."[144] The explosion of corruption during periods of military rule damaged the military's legitimacy as an institution and the related claims that it should govern in order to "clean up" Nigerian political life.[145]

In Nigeria, elected office has become one of the most effective ways of getting rich and gaining personal power.[146] In addition to outright theft, the elite also rig the system in their favor to the detriment of ordinary Nigerians and the economy by preventing repairs to government refineries, for example, to benefit vested interests in imported petroleum products, or by stalling power plants in order to profit from the sales of generators.[147] The traditional client-patron relationship in Nigerian societies lends itself to modern corruption, where, for instance in the north, "a powerful and wealthy feudal elite" held power for 200 years through patronage and appeal to religious sentiment.[148] Corruption is recognized for its ill effects, but official and civil society efforts to thwart it have frequently been opposed or circumvented. Even reform through religiously led struggle, or jihad for Muslims, has been co-opted, driving some Nigerians into more militant Islamic fundamentalism to combat this evil.[149] Poor economic conditions, lack of opportunity, and outright corruption all contribute to violence within Nigeria, often on a regional or ethnic basis.[150]

The dominance of petroleum in Nigeria's economy and politics has made the country subject to a single, internationally fluctuating source of income, has diminutized other sectors of the economy, and has made Nigeria one of the most politically unstable and corrupt states in the world.[151] In particular, the concentrated location of oil and accompanying natural gas deposits in (and increasingly off-shore) the fragile coastlands area of the Niger Delta had even more profound effects. This transformed the Delta into "one of the most intractable sources of political destabilization, [which] constitutes a profound threat to national security, and economic development of the Nigerian state."[152]

Problems in the Delta.

The Niger River Delta, the source of much of Nigeria's current wealth, consists of 9 of Nigeria's 36 states and occupies 12 percent of the country's territory. The core delta states of Bayelsa, Rivers, Delta, and Akwa Ibom have more than three-quarters of the onshore oil production and half of the regional population. The concentration of oil production and population has greatly degraded the environment, devastating local fishing and farming,[153] with little to no effective compensation. This results in the paradox that the Delta has Nigeria's lowest standard of living and suffers considerable environmental degradation from its rich hydrocarbon extraction.[154] Little has been done to counter the environmental despoliation caused by unfettered oil exploitation. Flaring of by-product natural gas also pollutes crops and air, and is destructive to wildlife. Farming and fishing grounds have been ruined, and gas flaring in the Delta is cited as Africa's single biggest contribution to greenhouse gas emissions.[155] The predominantly rural population, which consists of at least 40 different ethnic groups with perhaps 250 languages and dialects, has developed a common identity of being "Delta people," without a strong sense of being Nigerians. Cities like Warri, Port Harcourt, Sapele, and Ughelli have long since exceeded their carrying capacity and have little to no infrastructure.[156]

Responding to the destruction of their traditional economic and cultural base, much of the population at least passively supports a wide variety of armed criminal and political groups who kill for hire and target Western oil companies for extortion. Smuggling of stolen petroleum by sea in exchange for weapons as well as cash is endemic (and a significant cause of corruption in the Nigerian military).[157] Armed separatist groups repeatedly form and reform. Violent clashes have resulted in 1,500 deaths annually in the region and a destabilizing flow of internally displaced persons, adding to an already high rural to urban migration rate.[158] The Delta has become a significant fault line in Nigeria.[159] Paradoxically, it may also be a unifying factor, as the other regions appear unwilling to either lose the economic resources it controls or allow competing groups to gain complete control.

WHAT DIVIDES CAN UNITE

Despite its destructive role, both in the Delta and nationally, the oil economy is also a strong unifying factor, perhaps the most important at work in Nigeria today. Oil revenues distributed by the central government to Nigeria's states and provinces may be the most powerful of all incentives for unity among the many disparate economic, religious, ethnic, and regional groups. Each faction is beholden to the federal government for its share of the wealth, and with it resulting patronage, increase in government workers, and more central government control over the economy.[160] Ironically, the distribution of this wealth is often the cause of conflict among Nigerians, but, with better management, Nigerian oil revenues could be the key to stability and progress. The high economic growth rates recently achieved in Nigeria may be testament to the success of such improved management. As rising standards of living tend to reduce factionalism, the new economy and high oil prices reinforce long-established economic centripetal forces in keeping Nigerians working together.[161]

Despite its past of poor economic performance and rampant corruption, which have stunted and twisted Nigeria's economy to the detriment of many of its people, the economy remains the single most integrating force in Nigeria. With a history of regional specialization and resulting trade, respectable current economic growth, and vast natural resource wealth to boost economic and human development, Nigerians may see a brighter economic future together than apart—assuming that politics and communal strife do not intervene.

THE POLITICAL ECONOMY

The ultimate cause behind the regional, ethnic, and religious rivalries and conflict, made worse by previous colonial and federal government policies, may now be the struggle for control over Nigeria's wealth, mainly its petroleum income. Management of Nigeria's political economy (a broad concept that looks for economic motives behind political and social actions, and is concerned about "the interconnection of economic and political structures in social formation"[162]) may well decide Nigeria's future. Oxford University's Paul Collier explains that the primary motivation for conflicts are the opportunities to be gained from them, rather than the past grievances endured—meaning that regional, ethnic, or religious affiliations may be more the traits around which to organize to attain political economy ends rather than the real causes of violence.[163] This political economy explains in part why Nigeria is Balkanized today, with disputes exacerbated by institutional weaknesses, identity group rivalries in zero sum competition, and political corruption. The political economy is both Nigeria's most important centripetal and centrifugal factor, and its management will determine Nigeria's future unity.

Identity affiliations can be instrumentalized by groups to protect or enrich themselves through political power and economic resources, and cumulative bouts of violence make each instance of organizing such instruments easier.[164] The Berom, mainly Christian farmers from the central Plateau State, are an example of an ethnic minority who fear that weak connections and lack of patronage from the federal government allows dominant groups to displace them or despoil their lands with pollution from nearby tin mines. They organize as ethnic and economic groups to gain protection, autonomy, and control over resources.[165] Similar situations concerning the rights of indigenous minorities and migrants play out from the Niger Delta to northern Kaduna state creating some of Nigeria's largest and deadliest conflicts.[166] To alleviate such concerns, the federal government has granted larger minorities financial considerations for their loyalty to the government, and some have been granted their own states.[167]

Institutional deficiencies in Nigeria have abetted the scramble for resources and power. As noted earlier, poorly imposed Western structures and systems made indigenous methods and modern institutions dysfunctional.[168] In modern Nigeria, the inadequate condition of public services, policing, infrastructure, and the bureaucracy result in inequitable distribution of public goods and services. The dependence on and need for this public distribution, and its effect of corrupting officials and politicians, aggravates "social divisions and undermine[s] the legitimacy of government."[169] Organizing identity groups to protect minorities against dominating majority groups, of which the Berom are an example, is enshrined in Nigeria's constitution by which state and local governments may protect indigenous communities by discriminating against non-natives.[170]

However, competing claims to rights and entitlements create friction between groups where place of origin is more nebulous than the constitution envisions, and indigeneship contradicts other constitutional rights guaranteeing all Nigerians freedom from discrimination and freedom of movement.[171] For example, the Niger Delta violence occurs mainly because "Service delivery across the region is appalling and heavily compromised by patronage and corruption," despite this region having produced $200 billion in petroleum revenues for the federal government during the past decade.[172] Out of desperation, some Nigerians, especially the youth, resort to vigilantism or ethnic militias to supply policing where it is formally insufficient or go so far as violence and terrorism to attain their political or economic demands.[173] Unfortunately, the laws and structures in place to ensure regional and national protections and progress have been undermined since independence through poor implementation by Nigeria's elites who have proven venal, partisan, self-serving, and lacking in national political will.[174] Strong leadership can correct the problems of weak institutions, but Nigeria has none. This lack of strong national leadership encourages factionalism through indigeneship and competition for power and resources.

The constitution thus enables partisan leaders to exploit the compounding fractures in Nigerian society by organizing groups in self-serving, sometimes violent, ways. This is another cause of Balkanization in Nigeria and a tradition dating back to the British policy of divide and rule. Politics used for private ends to enjoy the wealth of public resources is widely prevalent in Nigeria.[175] Distribution of finite resources and wealth through political power is a zero sum competition among political elites who exacerbate their constituencies' differences for their own personal gain and to deflect attention from overall poor governance and economic conditions.[176] Political parties in Nigeria seem to organize to economically and politically advance their own elite by doling out patronage to clients in arrangements one author described as "Mafia-like associations."[177]

The instrumentalization of identity is apparent in the recurring crises in Plateau State's capital of Jos. Here fear that domination by Muslim Hausa-Fulani settlers would displace Christian indigenous elites from their privileged position motivated the use of the indigenous masses as "pawns on the chessboard of the political elite."[178] The expectation of access to lucrative powerful positions in government by the elite is rampant at state and federal levels and is a pillar of the zoning system described earlier.[179] Before their proliferation, state governments were fiscally self-sufficient, but since the 1960s, the power of states has grown relatively weaker as the size of their bureaucracies grew and they began to depend on federal subsidies.[180] What has not changed is the "desire of members of the political class for access to power and money," and need to control the federal government and its distribution of revenues that leads to deep regional antagonisms.[181]

The allocation of resource revenues from the federal government is probably the central point around which ethnic groups contend, shifting the distribution formula based on who holds power. States that produce most of Nigeria's revenues have been able to extract more funds for their development, "the derivation principle." These funds have grown from 3 percent in the early 1990s to 18 percent, although they are still not the level of 20-25 percent sought. Some groups use threats of violence to gain political and economic strength. Ethnically and regionally organized groups, like the Movement for the Emancipation of the Niger Delta (MEND), curbed Nigeria's petroleum output by about 25 percent through violence in 2006, driving in part changes in revenue distributions.[182] This is a successful example of a common method by which groups "use violence so that they can gain greater favor from the government."[183] Nigeria's political economy is a lucrative resource divided among its elites who mobilize identity groups based on ethnicity, religious, and regional affiliations although those mobilized masses more often insufficiently benefit from their participation.

Weak institutions and mobilization of identity groups are often exploited by Nigeria's ruling class for their own selfish benefit. Political and economic corruption, then, may be the origin of the fighting over the political economy, and the violence derailing further Nigerian unity and development. Economic gains from holding office are the primary motivation of politics in Nigeria.[184] Distorted traditional forms of the client-patron relationship have co-opted constituents of politicians, civil servants, and the military into making political corruption a venue by which connected Nigerians are enriched. Voters are often convinced that they gain when their identity groups benefit by the actions of politicians, and are mobilized to their service—legitimate and otherwise.[185]

The enriched elite and their associates, then, must protect their power to continue to derive these benefits. Thus, to maintain political position, corruption in modern Nigeria has been essential through electoral fraud, killing and imprisoning opposition members, use of violence and intimidation, extortion and outright stealing to name just some methods.[186] Nigerian elites employ competing identity groups to ensure the future of their power and economic bases, and address their constituents' "political anxiety" and "collective fears of the future," which the elites callously create or reinforce.[187] Unfortunately, the perception that the masses in these identity groups benefit from factional politics is misplaced, because the greed and lack of accountability of its leaders, especially at the state and local levels, leave little to trickle down. This accounts for the miserable state of the Niger Delta communities despite billions in revenue now allocated to these states.[188] Since the elite depend on resource distributions rather than taxes for funds needed for governing and their illicit personal revenues, they have grown dismissive of their constituents except when needed to mobilize in support of the elite's interests.[189] Local militias and terrorist groups, like MEND and Boko Haram, are a reaction against the corruption of local ethnic and religious elites. Their aim is to gain more control of power and resources for the constituents rather than their corrupt representatives and leaders.[190] Economic and political corruption by Nigerian elites has hijacked the political economy of Nigeria, leaving in its wake a fractured and impoverished country and a roiling citizenry.

Despite its complex past, reason for hope remains for unity among Nigerians, especially as the Fourth Republic matures politically. Historian Adiele Afigbo believed Nigerian unity could be rebuilt through the lessons of its pre-colonial histories, in which differing ethnic, religious, regional, economic, and political groups complemented one another and settled differences more constructively than today, although not conflict free.[191] Recent political events also may indicate that Nigeria's fractious past is ending, with four consecutive elections for executives with successful transfers of power and the 2011 poll showing a marked improvement over previous ones, as signs of cooperation. The election in 2011 of President Jonathan, a minority Ijaw from the impoverished Niger Delta state of Bayelsa, may be a welcome change from business as usual.[192] As Nigerian citizens experience the current federal political system, they are gaining a more tolerant view of its workings, even among skeptical northern Nigerians.[193] The single strongest factor in preserving Nigeria is perhaps that no powerful group, from the military to the minorities, seriously wants to dismember Nigeria, all seeing the economic advantages of unity, even while fighting over its spoils.[194] Nigeria today hangs in balance with unity or devolution both possible. The result depends upon how its leaders guide Nigeria through its crises and manage its extreme and violent elements.

FAULT LINES

Nigeria already possesses the characteristics of a shatter belt, the fracturing of a region under persistent stress from external forces. Parochial interests created by religious, cultural, ethnic, economic, regional, and political secessionist tendencies, as outlined herein, are endemic in Nigeria. Under such stresses, Nigerian unity may fail. Should Nigeria's leaders mismanage the political economy and reinforce centrifugal forces in Nigeria, the breaks to create autonomous regions or independent countries would likely occur along its previously identified fault lines.[195] Having already experienced one brutal civil war, Nigeria is at risk for a recurrence of conflict or dissolution, especially since some of the underpinning motivations of the war remain unresolved.[196] From 1999 to 2006, 14,000 Nigerians were killed across the country, and three million Nigerians were displaced in intercommunal clashes.[197]

Should Nigerians be unable "to reconcile the imperatives of nationhood with entrenched regional, ethnic, and religious identities," they could split under conditions similar to recent successions in Indonesia, Ethiopia, and Yugoslavia, or the de facto break in Somalia.[198] Indeed, East Timor, Eritrea, Croatia, and Somaliland indicate that the weakest point of failing states is along relict colonial borders. Each of these contiguous states was administered separately by different colonial masters before being poorly merged together prior or subsequent to independence. Of more interest for Nigerian unity is that this may also occur between regions separately administered by a common colonial power as occurred between Malaysia and Singapore, and North and South Sudan, where differences proved irreconcilable after the departure of British administration. At least some of the resulting regions and states of a possible Nigerian devolution may divide along such internal lines.

Although the two protectorates that formed modern Nigeria formally existed for only short periods (14 years from 1900 for the north, and 8 years from 1906 for the south), they themselves were formed from earlier autonomous protectorates (the Colony and Protectorate of Lagos to the west, a smaller Protectorate of Southern Nigeria to the east extending westward across the Niger River to include modern Ebo state, and a very recognizable Protectorate of Northern Nigeria).[199] This north-south colonial border represents a myriad of persistent physical and human differences in Nigeria that endure today as a relict political boundary. As early as 1905, the northern border of southern Nigeria was delimited by the British as a straight line from the German Kamerun border 10 miles south of Takum due west to Ida through then uncharted territory, to follow westward the approximate northern borders of present day states Edo, Ondo, Ekiti, Osun, and Oyo.[200] Although this line has been adjusted subsequently to reflect better knowledge and evolving circumstances, its essence has remained little changed to the current era.[201]

The two protectorates that joined to form the 1906 Protectorate of Southern Nigeria are also important in any possible future devolution story because they approximate a second fault line in modern Nigeria along the Niger River and its Delta, which demarcates the traditional areas of the Yoruba and Igbo. The western Lagos protectorate was acquired by the British in 1861 and grew in size until 1886 when the territory was first administered directly from Lagos itself. After the Berlin Conference in 1885, the British established the separate Oil Rivers Protectorate spanning from the Niger Delta to Old Calabar. In 1893, this protectorate was expanded westward to the Lagos protectorate and northward to the Niger River port city of Idah (Ida or Idda) 40 miles south of Lokoja, approximating the later boundaries of the 1906 Protectorate of Southern Nigeria. Unlike the territorial self-government of Lagos, however, the Protectorate of Southern Nigeria was administered directly from the Colonial Office in London.[202] The 1906 amalgamation of southern Nigeria proved fleeting, however, when in 1939 the British split it again along the Niger River, confirming the deep differences between the more urban and centrally organized Yoruba as the Western Province, and the village-oriented sub-tribal stage of development of Sobo, Igbo, and Ibibio Eastern Province.[203] Again colonial administration reflected traditional differences that persisted in manifesting themselves throughout Nigeria's history and started a long sequence of fracturing in Nigerian political states.

In turn, these early colonial regions reflected closely the outline of 19th century pre-colonial states and peoples with the Fulani Sokoto Caliphate and Bornu Kingdom to the north; Igbo, Ibibio, and related peoples' communities to the east; and a collection of Yoruba dominated states to the west, including the Kingdoms of Benin and Warri. Only the Igala, Idoma, Tiv, and Jukun people along the south bank of the Benue River were outside of the 1960 Northern Region to which they would be a part.[204] Early British administrators recognized the divergent interests of these western, eastern, and northern regions, but were compelled to merge them because the northern protectorate could not economically sustain itself. In one form or another, these internal regional boundaries proved durable for a century.

The administrative lines that separated the protectorates also roughly demarcate a series of other physical and human differences within Nigeria that have sharply delineated its people, as outlined throughout this monograph. Physical geography, which is the foundation for human activities such as agriculture, housing structures, settlement patterns, and other cultural activities helped to form the different regional, ethnic, and cultural groupings in Nigeria. Such groups may complement each other, adding to Nigeria's diversity and strength through trade, diplomacy, and diffusion of ideas, as often occurred in the region's pre-colonial history.[205] However, if the differences are mismanaged or accentuated for political reasons or personal gain, such groupings could become the entities around which to rally in defense of perceived and antithetical group interests, as may occur in political economy disputes.

The lines of division were recognized in 1939 when three divisions were officially constituted by the British as the Eastern, Western, and Northern Provinces with strong regional governments organized differently in order to allow governing to reflect each separate heritage. These divisions were along significant internal borders that separated Yoruba affiliated people to the southwest, from Igbo affiliated people in the southeast, and from the Hausa-Fulani people in the north. This attempt at federalism was insufficient to prevent further Balkanization within independent Nigeria. It eventually fragmented into 36 states. Within this subsequent fragmentation, the north-east-west internal borders running as described remained virtually unaltered. They continued to act as powerful psychological borders and fault lines.

The perseverance of such fault lines is due to the endurance of the underlying factors that caused them. The identity and history associated with these divides make them a convenient rallying point for the disaffected and threatened. Such was the case in 1967 when the people of the southeast, led by the Igbo, seceded from Nigeria as Biafra in the disastrous civil war. Here the differences in peoples and regions were not just theoretical, but a manifest reality in which one-half to two million people died,[206] emphasizing the significance of such divisions in devolution. Recent conflict between Christians and Muslims in Nigeria reminds us that the north-south border could be another fracture point.

These geographic fault lines are reinforced in Nigeria by easy to obtain public resources, such as oil, which make a rentier state more prone to secessionist movements. This is especially true when the resource is spatially concentrated and the economy dependent upon it, but its economic impact to the source region would be diluted through sharing with others in the country. Not only does this help to explain why recently discovered oil spurred Biafra to secede, but also why other ethnic groups such as the Ibibio, Efik, and Sobo acquiesced to the Igbo effort. The most obvious reason for secession was that Igbos were attacked in the north in 1967, although not the other natives from the southeast. However, economic control over a lucrative resource is a powerful incentive to create a political community within a contiguous, if ethnically diverse, region, especially if the resource may then finance the rebellion as occurred in Nigeria's southeast.[207]

Before the civil war started, however, a different arrangement in Nigerian politics further illustrates this point. Before 1965, Nigeria's main source of income and major export was cocoa, produced in the southwest by the Yoruba. Then Nigerian politics was dominated by a northern and southeastern alliance in order to receive their share of cocoa revenue. "The discovery of oil . . . destroyed the rationale for this political alignment. Very rapidly, a new coalition formed between the North and the South-West against the oil rich South-East."[208] In Nigeria today, a cultural and political entity is developing in the Niger Delta among the many groups that see themselves as "Delta People,"[209] in reaction to their powerlessness over the rape of their environment and worst standard of living in Nigeria despite being the source of the country's oil wealth. The region is more geographically compact and resource rich than Biafra and hosts Nigeria's only serious, if currently dormant, liberation movements in the Nigerian Delta People's Volunteer Force and MEND.[210]

The divides painted in broad brush here are not as sharp as presented. The Middle Belt, the southern band of the old northern protectorate,[211] is a transition area of cultures, physical geographic influences, and allegiances that encompasses 180 native ethnic groups and defies easy assignment to the Northern Region and its colonial and Islamic predecessor territories, since the Middle Belt was never fully absorbed by them.[212] The border is just as indistinct in the Niger River delta where not only is the river hard to define, but also the many overlapping tribes are difficult to categorize into Yorubaland or Igboland. The cosmopolitan nature of Nigeria's cities and some of its regions, such as the northeast, represents all manner of religious, ethnic, cultural, economic, and other affiliations from across Nigeria.

Although indistinct lines and intermingling of allegiances and economic interests in Nigeria make devolution difficult and unattractive, these factors do not make it impossible. India and Pakistan split after independence in 1947 under similar circumstances with a bloody partition, followed by decades of intermittent war fueled by political, religious, and ethnic interests. The difficulty of a Nigerian split, should it occur, and the economic stakes involved, may predetermine that it will also be violent, as the two Sudans are demonstrating.

Forced migration could also solve the problems of intermingled peoples of different allegiances and indefinite boundary lines in Nigeria. In Nigeria, the history of what is now referred to as ethnic cleansing goes back over 200 years, as seen in the original establishment of some Yoruba cities as war time refugee camps. Ethnic cleansing was rampant during the Nigerian civil war when over two million Igbos fled east to Biafra, escaping retribution for the Igbo-led military coup attempt that precipitated the civil war.[213] Recent bouts of ethnic and especially religious conflict in northern Nigeria has already begun to force minorities out of cities. Thus, classic lines for violent devolution exist in Nigeria, exacerbated by many regional differences.

SOLUTIONS

What is Being Done? The Nigerian Response.

To avoid devolution, the Nigerian government has managed centrifugal forces through a variety of means. They have encouraged a sense of national consciousness through the use of inclusive nationalist symbols ranging from use of the flag and the common currency, to the bold step of relocating the capital from the South's Lagos to the more central location of Abuja.[214] More substantially, since economic well-being and open responsive political systems are important to citizens to avert civil conflict and splintering,[215] there have been significant efforts to improve the economic well-being of Nigerians as a whole and make the Nigerian government more effective and responsive.

Nigerian anti-corruption measures have had some positive effect. The government has recently implemented more market-oriented reforms to the economy along International Monetary Fund requirements, and has begun a public-private program to improve power generation and distribution, and road networks.[216] Strong economic growth averaging over 7 percent GDP expansion during the past decade also helps to contribute to economic well-being despite deeply rooted centrifugal forces, as was also true of Yugoslavia from the 1950s to 1970s in overcoming the intrastate ethnic horrors perpetrated during World War II.

Politically, there is also hope for the unity of Nigeria in its legal and power sharing arrangements. Civil society is still active and the legal establishment has been surprisingly effective. The Nigerian Supreme Court, for example, has played an important role in preserving the federal system by balancing the demands of the states vis-à-vis the central government.[217] The ruling party often brings smaller opposition groups together under a "big tent," offering incentives for cooperation and stability. This use of negotiation to share power has significantly restrained the use of violence, which would otherwise be the only method of obtaining power by competing political blocs.[218]

Ethnic and regional power brokering (such as the de facto rotation of the top six federal government posts among different groups) and repeated structural changes to the constitution and the government have acted as both centrifugal and centripetal forces. They have helped temporarily alleviate regional and ethnic tensions. They also weaken the long-term legitimacy of the state, however, by making it more the result and object of elite power brokering, which effectively excludes marginalized groups. This undercuts other claims of state legitimacy, such as representation of national interests or popular support.

What Is to Be Done? The U.S. Role.

Since the fate of Nigeria is an important national interest to the United States, the U.S. Government should engage with Nigerians to assist, as it best may, with improving Nigeria's stability and prosperity, and supporting its sovereign integrity. U.S. interests, as described in the opening section of this monograph, would be damaged to varying degrees by Nigeria's collapse into a collection of successor states. U.S. action alone will not preserve Nigeria, as centripetal and centrifugal forces are deeply rooted in Nigerian society. Nigeria's future will be decided on the ability of Nigerians to successfully manage their political economy, sustain centripetal forces, and contain centrifugal forces.

Small Foot, Big Footprint.

By using the low cost, nonintrusive approach outlined here that strengthens centripetal forces in Nigeria, the United States can reinforce an important strategic partner that "has consistently bent but never broke."[219] U.S. efforts should be aimed at strengthening institutions that can build a unified Nigeria and mitigate the damage if Nigeria splinters by making successor states more viable. These efforts should include expanding the U.S. diplomatic presence, supporting anticorruption measures at the top and bottom, improving the quality of non-partisan and technical advice to government officials, and focusing and enhancing security cooperation activities.

Nigeria's wealth and deep political involvement in international affairs greatly insulate it from outside pressure.[220] However, the United States can significantly assist Nigerian efforts by focusing on key issues where the United States has particular strengths and interests at stake. This would include the central issue of the management of the political economy where the United States can play a useful role with a whole of government approach helping develop the institutional and physical infrastructure necessary for the state and the economy to function. This should not be taken as a recommendation to increase the absolute value of U.S. assistance to Nigeria. Nigeria is already the second largest recipient of U.S. bilateral foreign assistance in Sub-Saharan Africa, following only Kenya.[221] However, new targeted low cost measures would be useful and should make existing programs more successful.

To be effective, a whole of government approach is necessary. The unified combatant command for the region, U.S. African Command (AFRICOM), with its declared intention of integrating the expertise of military and civilian officials, should spur the creation of an interagency coordinating group, specifically focused on Nigeria, as similar focused groups have been created for countries(such as Iraq and the Philippines) facing similar challenges to national unity with similar implications for U.S. interests. The chair of this coordinating group should have sufficient stature to represent the United States or participate in the U.S.-Nigeria Binational Commission, other bilateral groups, and international donor conferences. The formation of such a group would signal recognition of Nigeria's increasing importance to policymakers just as the creation of AFRICOM was intended to signal U.S. recognition of Africa's increasing strategic importance in 2007.[222]

Security Assistance.

As part of a unified, whole of government U.S. strategy, security assistance can be particularly useful in a country where the military is traditionally influential. Nigeria has received counterterrorism assistance from the United States, including $2.2 million for the development of a counterterrorism infantry company and $6.2 million aimed at building the capacity of the counterterrorism unit and tactical communications interoperability. The United States should also consider more fully supporting the counterinsurgency oriented approach President Jonathan has taken in the Delta. His amnesty and jobs program has seriously weakened existing rebel groups. This is in contrast to the more counterterrorism oriented approach taken by the Nigerian government with respect to Boko Haram. For instance, seizing the close relatives of alleged members clearly seems to have produced actionable intelligence for further raids on Boko Haram cadre. However, it has not addressed the causes for Boko Haram's rise and will likely spur more revenge attacks. Boko Haram itself grew out of the forcible suppression of an earlier, similar movement.

Nevertheless, Boko Haram has increased the level of sophistication in its attacks and expanded the range of attacks southward despite the fact that it has little appeal to non-Northerners.[223] If this trend continues, the United States should consider using its own intelligence capabilities to better target Boko Haram's leadership. However, the elimination of Boko Haram's leadership by any element could have permanent effects only if there is a corresponding effort to address the more fundamental centrifugal forces outlined herein that create the political space in which Boko Haram and any likely successor organization operate.

In and Out of the Delta.

To support the more broadly based counterinsurgency approach that the Nigerian government is apparently using in the Delta, which is designed to reduce the conditions that cause insurgencies, the Department of Defense (DoD) should offer organizational and logistical support through its U.S. Army Corps of Engineers for infrastructure construction that both enhances security and creates mass employment opportunities. Successful projects should at least temporarily reduce the number of the local unemployed who have formed a recruiting pool for the armed militias. The United States should also be willing to provide direct security protection for such projects, where Nigerian forces are unable to do so. While Western oil companies have been willing to fund such infrastructure projects in the Delta, adequate technical and management of logistical support has been difficult to obtain due to the security situation.

Given the scale of U.S. interests in the region and its obvious importance to Nigeria, the United States and Nigeria should jointly commit themselves to forming a coordinated strategy for Delta regional development, which should include the multidonor Niger Delta Planning Group, civil society, and the private sector.[224] Although numerous plans for regional development projects already exist, many of which have integrated local input, few have been implemented to any effect.[225] Vigorous United States support for plans that have already been created locally and with local input, incorporated into a coordinated strategy with Nigerian government support, could have a powerful, energizing effect while insulating the United States against charges of foreign interference. A similar approach should be taken in other troubled regions, such as Central Plateau State.

This kind of approach, using the U.S. Army Corps of Engineers, could be especially important in terms of road construction in other key regions, such as Central Plateau State. Passable roads foster local commerce, particularly small farm-based agricultural commerce, and tie the regions together. Of course, they also make it possible for Nigeria's security forces to operate. Unfortunately, since 1991, Nigeria has lost 31,500 kilometers (km) of paved road, which has deteriorated into gravel (although petroleum is the major component of asphalt). Other key infrastructure that helps keep Nigeria together is similarly neglected. The once well-run railroad system has declined dramatically. Nigerian ports are among the least efficient in the world due to poor government management policies and lack of support.[226] Much of the deterioration is due to local bandits or other armed groups and an absence of an effective government presence. U.S. security assistance, with possible additional technical and management support, for such infrastructure projects would greatly reinforce the forces that hold Nigeria together. Both the existing National Guard linkage and the new U.S. regional brigade for West Africa should be used along with Nigerian forces on such projects. This would also create the opportunity for expanded training on peacekeeping operations for Nigerian troops who will be deployed outside the country on peacekeeping operations. It would also give American forces valuable expertise in West Africa.

Although such projects would have a developmental effect, they should be seen and managed as security assistance projects that are part of an integrated counterinsurgency approach. Such a cohesive approach would best be coordinated, if not managed, by AFRI-COM. It is the U.S. organization best equipped to lead a broadly based counterinsurgency strategy.

Into the Regions.

Although the fate of the country will likely be decided by internal tensions, the United States has had little contact with, and even less understanding of, the regions outside of the former capital, Lagos, and the current capital, Abuja. Since Nigerian fault lines are regionally and ethnically based, the United States should make every effort to understand the regions beyond these cities. Opening or reopening small U.S. Embassy posts in Nigeria's three most important regional center cities, the North's Kano, the Southwest's Ibadan, and the Southeast's Port Harcourt, would allow the United States to acquire direct knowledge of critical regions and issues along Nigeria's geographic fault lines. It would be especially important that they reach out to local religious leaders with whom there has been little to no contact. Such mini-posts should have "regional military attachés" to liaise with regional Nigerian commands. To make best use of these positions, service as a "regional military attaché" should be tied to assignments in AFRICOM.

An important function of such officers would be to identify Nigerians who could participate in expanded training and exchange programs, including the International Fellows Program at the U.S. Army War College. After their posting, these officers would also bring back first-hand knowledge to the staffs and commands to which they are assigned.

Without a sustained presence, it is difficult to see how the United States can expect to understand local dynamics or forge relationships with regional leaders.

This is particularly important as the most prominent threats to both Nigeria's future and U.S. interests are regionally based. The continuing conflict in Plateau State and the city of Jos, the attacks on oil installations in the Delta, and Boko Haram's sectarian attacks are all examples of regionally based threats that have implications for Nigeria's future as a state. This proposal is a relatively low cost, high-visibility way to show U.S. interest in Nigeria and its people, while learning what policies the United States can best adopt to protect its interests.

Corruption.

Corruption, particularly petroleum-related corruption, is a central cause of the weakening of the Nigerian state at all levels. It is also an obvious issue for the United States to help address. The Nigerian government has had some success with anticorruption measures that should be taken further by the United States. Technical assistance by U.S. anti-fraud units to the relatively new Sovereign Wealth Fund to better manage petroleum revenue could also be very effective.[227] This type of assistance is only lightly intrusive on internal Nigerian affairs, but offers the benefits of making officials more honest in their dealings and returns a larger percentage of Nigeria's annual wealth back to government control.

While trying to throttle demand for smuggled oil, the United States can also help reduce the ability of smugglers to transport and sell stolen oil. Successful Nigerian crackdowns on piracy and smuggling have caused pirates and smugglers to operate further along the West African coast in international waters beyond the range of Nigerian patrol boats. Nigeria has been given modest amounts of training and equipment for its coastal forces by the United States. However, both coastal and maritime capacities are limited. A similar lack of capacity and regional cooperation in the area as a whole means that there is currently little prospect of a comprehensive regional strategy.[228] With good relations with the countries involved, the United States should make efforts to help forge a regional interdiction strategy, with possible additional support to both Nigeria and neighboring Gulf of Guinea countries. As a third party, the United States can play a useful role as an "honest broker" in forging a regional agreement for interdiction in the Gulf, with some degree of assistance and support eventually required from the U.S. Coast Guard and Navy.

As part of this effort, the United States should support Nigerian initiatives to develop and use oil tagging (chemical identity marking of oil at its point of origin) and a certification scheme to track the theft and sale of "blood oil" in order to control smuggling and corruption from bunkering.[229] Combined with expanded technical assistance to Nigerian and foreign financial institutions to track ill-gotten wealth, this has the potential to help remove a major source of funding for weapons by separatist groups in the Delta and help reduce the possibility of arms smuggling. By reducing demand and degrading the ability of smugglers to transport stolen oil, this approach should increase the flow of legitimate oil into the world market as well as the flow of legitimate revenue to the Nigerian government.

As much of the arms and oil smuggling is done through the Delta itself, a land presence will be required. Much of the Delta has no government military or police presence. Here again, use of the regionally aligned brigade to train local forces for security and police duties in what is essentially a domestic peacekeeping operation would be extremely helpful. AFRICOM's insistence on the importance of civilian protection in this kind of operation would be especially valuable for a long-term solution for this critical region.

Soft Power.

As noted, the U.S. funded Carnegie Corporation-Nigerian cooperative project of the 1950s was used successfully to help build a common Nigerian national consciousness. However, there has been no sustained follow-up, and the declining educational system has become a priority target for groups such as Boko Haram. To strengthen this important centripetal force, the United States should encourage the formation of a new cooperative program between Nigeria and private U.S. institutions to similarly reform Nigeria's educational curriculum for the 21st century. Combined with an expanded academic exchange program at the university level, this could have profound effects over the long term in shaping a national consciousness and perhaps intercultural tolerance. This should be linked with an expanded AFRICOM supported exchange and curriculum reform program supporting the same values within Nigeria's military and security-related training institutes, such as the Nigerian Defence Academy and the National Institute of Policy and Strategic Studies.

In a similar fashion, the United States should fund and support a cooperative project to establish a robust interfaith dialogue between Christians and Muslims. Although there have been several attempts by Christians and Muslims in Nigeria to improve relations and reduce violence, they have tended to fade out over time. The United States has a well-established tradition of organizing more enduring interfaith linkages and programs and could be a useful third-party intermediary in building on these Nigerian-led efforts. Unlike Nigerian government agencies, the United States is not perceived as captured or dominated by various regional power blocs. It can therefore supply political cover to independent Nigerian efforts, serving as an honest broker and funder. The United States Institute of Peace-supported Interfaith Mediation Center, a joint Christian–Muslim effort, has already had success in resolving conflicts between Christians and Muslims in the Middle Belt and in the North.[230] U.S. support for Nigerian-led efforts, exercised through experienced private and quasigovernmental American institutions seen as neither Christian nor Muslim, would be very helpful. Through such means, the United States could build a national mediation network based in the regions, while establishing useful ties to Nigeria's religious institutions. Given the importance AFRICOM attaches to local conflict resolution in peacekeeping operations, it would seem useful to form linkages with mediation centers. Assistance to resolution of local religiously-linked disputes, whether it is done through engineering, agricultural, or security support, have proven time and again to be critical in restoring peace to troubled regions from the Philippines to the Balkans. Assistance offered by the regionally aligned brigade and National Guard operations, in conjunction with the Nigerian military with which military-to-military linkages already exist, would be useful in themselves and offer peacekeeping training that would be useful in any context.

Governance.

While there are extraordinarily talented individuals within the Nigerian civil service, the government as a whole often lacks the managerial depth to fully manage the political economy. This is most telling in Parliament, which is the only place where all regional and ethnic groups have a chance to be represented, but which often lacks the technical capacity to fully analyze its decisions. Helping Nigerians train and resource nonpartisan parliamentary staff and institutions, such as the equivalent of the U.S. Congressional Budget Office and the Congressional Research Service, would be enormously useful. Similar programs throughout the civil service, focused on management and technical areas, could help revitalize the once proud civil service that was damaged during the periods of authoritarian rule. Including Nigerian civilian government executives in strategic studies programs, such as those at one of the colleges at the National Defense University (NDU), would support both better understanding by key Nigerian civilian leaders and strengthen productive civil-military relations with the Nigerian officers attending these programs. The Nigerian government currently does not send civilian government defense leaders to NDU, but they do to the Africa Center for Strategic Studies (ACSS) Senior Leaders Seminar, where select Nigerian military and civilian leaders meet with equivalent U.S. and other African leaders for 2 weeks of illuminating frank discussions on important African security issues. The ACSS Next Generation of African Security Sector Leaders Course does the same thing for mid-level leaders. Focusing on rebuilding or strengthening services to existing leaders and institutions should make assistance more acceptable and effective in practice.

AFRICOM.

In sum, the United States should take a whole of government approach in forming a strategy for Nigeria. The DoD would play a key role, most notably through AFRICOM, in this unified U.S. effort.

As part of a broad effort of internal peace building with the Nigerian government, the DoD should offer organizational and logistical support through its U.S. Army Corps of Engineers for infrastructure construction that enhances security, diversifies and strengthens the economy, and creates mass employment opportunities. However, unless the United States commits to a foreign internal defense stance in Nigeria, which seems doubtful and Nigerian acceptance of a foreign operational force within its borders even more so, coordination among U.S. agencies, NGOs and international government organizations (IGOs), and major U.S. and other national corporations already in Nigeria would be the best way to enhance economic development. In some parts of Nigeria, security remains a major obstacle. However, this obstacle could be defused by convincing the federal government to partner in meaningful consultation and execution of such cooperative efforts with local societal groups, governments, and economic organizations. Recent U.S. experience with stability operations in Iraq and Afghanistan makes the DoD an informed and experienced participant within the interagency and international effort, but caution must be exercised regarding which lessons are applied. They must also be done in a way that complements the complexities of the Nigerian environment. The U.S.-Nigeria Binational Commission may be the best venue to bring together the

United States, Nigeria, NGOs, and private ventures for coordination and implementation, since two of its priority topics are economic and infrastructure development and social service delivery.

To foster a unified approach, AFRICOM should lead the creation of an interagency coordinating group, specifically focused on Nigeria and threats to its national unity. AFRICOM already has ties and liaisons to all of the major U.S. agencies involved in Sub-Saharan Africa, as well as better staff and resources with which to manage an interagency effort. However, in this role, AFRICOM may best be used as a behind the scenes "back room staff" supporting and coordinating the work of the State Department, the U.S. Agency for International Development (USAID), and other agencies to keep a civilian face on U.S. Government involvement.

The interagency coordinating group effort should include in its focus Nigeria-based or related transnational security threats in West Africa. Here the military's natural focus and lessons learned from experiences in Iraq and Afghanistan will be informative. Using this group to augment U.S. engagement through the Binational Commission is appropriate, given its focus on Nigeria's regional security role and recent bilateral discussions on security in the crucial Niger Delta region.

As part of this coordinated effort, AFRICOM should use the U.S. regional brigade for West Africa to expand linkages and build institutional memory of issues and processes that both Nigerians and Americans consider important. This should be done by building upon the existing Nigerian military and California National Guard relations. Training local forces for security and police duties to professionalize their efforts and legitimize their use in the eyes of their citizens would be an important advance in Nigeria's stability. Assuming a U.S.-supported regional agreement for oil and weapons smuggling interdiction in the Gulf of Guinea, AFRICOM should use the U.S. regionally aligned brigade to train local forces in land-based interdiction, and the Coast Guard could do the same for maritime. However, Nigerian sensitivities might dictate that such training not occur in Nigeria, or at least only in a classroom. However, such opportunities would also provide the regionally aligned brigade with valuable cultural understanding and a meaningful exchange with a force that has also conducted peace and stability operations in which both sides may learn from each other. Additionally, AFRICOM should expand its exchanges with Nigeria's military and security-related training institutes and assist with their curriculum and institutional reform. This should be coupled with the broader suggested effort focused on civilian institutions. AFRICOM, and other U.S. DoD-related institutions, should include civilian Nigerian government executives in expanded strategic studies exchange programs.

CONCLUSION

Nigeria's future as a unified entity is under threat along distinct and identifiable fault lines. These threats are reflections of internally generated centrifugal forces that compete with the counterbalancing centripetal forces that have held Nigeria together since it was formed. However, new factors have greatly frayed the Nigerian union. Religion has increasingly become more divisive in Nigeria and has exacerbated tension along the fault lines. The concentration of vast petroleum wealth has exercised a tremendous disruptive force on the economy and the government. The explosive growth of corruption may well hollow out the Nigerian state as it destroys the economic and political systems that support it. Nevertheless, there are powerful centripetal forces at work. Regional and ethnic groups fear domination by other neighboring groups without the protection of a unified state. The Biafran War and local clashes have made clear the potential cost of separation. For most groups, it is still more economically advantageous to share in the larger national economy. Long-standing cultural, historical, and economic ties still bind the country together. Although not yet robust, there has been an evolution of a national consciousness within a common historical experience and a shared English-speaking culture.

If centrifugal forces triumph over centripetal forces, U.S. interests will be damaged. Under grave threat of devolution, Nigeria's integrity and prosperity are not only possible, but also can be positively influenced with judicious U.S. policies and should be a priority for U.S. policymakers. Although Nigeria's fate is primarily in Nigerian hands, it can be positively affected by American actions. Nigeria's future is in balance and the United States should help tip the scales. By helping Nigerians protect Nigerian interests, it will help protect its own.

BIBLIOGRAPHY

Abdullahi, Salisu A. "Ethnicity and Ethnic Relations in Nigeria: The Case of Religious Conflict in Kano" in Judy Carter, George Irani, and Vamik D. Volkan, eds., *Regional and Ethnic Conflicts: Perspectives from the Front Lines*. Upper Saddle River, NJ: Pearson Prentice Hall, 2009, pp. 292-299.

Adebajo, Adekeye. *The Curse of Berlin: Africa After the Cold War*. New York: Columbia University Press, 2010.

Adesoji, Abimbola O. "Between Maitatsine and Boko Haram: Islamic Fundamentalism and the Response of the Nigerian State." *Africa Today*, Vol. 57, No. 4, Summer 2011, pp. 98-119.

Albert, Isaac O. "Communication in the Escalation of Ethnic and Religious Conflict" in Ernest E. Uwaizie, Isaac O. Albert, and Godfrey N. Uzoigwe, eds., *Inter-Ethnic and Religious Conflict Resolution in Nigeria*. Lanham, MD: Lexington Books, 1999, pp. 19-36.

Albert, Isaac O. "The Sociocultural Politics of Ethnic and Religious Conflicts" in Ernest E. Uwaizie, Isaac O. Albert, and Godfrey N. Uzoigwe, eds., *Inter-Ethnic and Religious Conflict Resolution in Nigeria*. Lanham, MD: Lexington Books, 1999, pp. 70-87.

Allen, Fidelis and Ufo Okeke-Uzodike. "Oil, Politics, and Conflict in the Niger Delta: A Nonkilling Analysis." *Africa Peace and Conflict Journal*, Vol. 3, No. 2, pp. 32-42. Available from *www.humansecuritygateway.com/documents/APCJ_Vol3No2Dec2010.pdf*.

Alozieuwa, Simeon H. O. "Beyond the Ethno-Religious Theory of the Jos Conflict." *Africa Peace and Conflict Journal*, Vol. 3, No. 2, pp. 18-31. Available from *www.humansecuritygateway.com/documents/APCJ_Vol3No2Dec2010.pdf*.

American School of International Service. "The Biafran War," Washington DC: American University School of International Service, November 1997. Available from *www1.american.edu/ted/ice/biafra.htm*.

Asuni, Judith. *Special Report: Blood Oil in the Niger Delta*. Washington, DC: United States Institute of Peace, August 2009.

Atoh, Samuel Aryeetey. "Africa South of the Sahara" in Douglas S. Johnson, Viola Haarmann, Merrill L. Johnson, and David L. Clawson, eds., *World Regional Geography*. Upper Saddle Brook, NJ: Pearson Prentice Hall, 2010, pp. 400-465.

Ayodele, Bonnie. "Silence on Climate Change and Natural Resources Conflict in Nigeria: The Niger Delta Region Experience" in Donald Anthony Mwiturubani and Jo-Ansie van Wyk, eds., *Climate Change and Natural Resources Conflicts in Africa*. Pretoria, South Africa: Institute for Security Studies, 2010, pp. 105-122. Available from *www.humansecuritygateway.com/documents/ ISS_ClimateChangeandNaturalResourcesConflictsinAfica.pdf*.

Benedict, Akpomuvie Orhioghene. "Breaking Barriers to Transformation of the Niger Delta Region of Nigeria: A Human Development Paradigm." *Journal of Sustainable Development*, Vol. 4, No. 3, June 2011, pp. 210-221.

Blessing, Michael A. *Nigeria's Center(s) of Gravity: A Complex and Violent Operational Environment*. Carlisle, PA: U.S. Army War College, 2008. Available from *www.dtic.mil/cgi-bin/GetTRDoc?AD =ADA478387&Location=U2&doc=GetTRDoc.pdf*.

Bradley, Matthew Todd. "Inter-Ethnic Antagonism in Post-Colonial Nigeria: Ethnicity vs. Symbolic Nationalism." *Journal of Cultural Studies*, Vol. 7, No. 1, 2006.

Casey, Conerly. "Mediated Hostility, Generation, and Victimhood in Northern Nigeria," in Judy Carter, George Irani, and Vamik D. Volkan, eds., *Regional and Ethnic Conflicts: Perspectives from the Front Lines*. Upper Saddle River, NJ: Pearson Prentice Hall, 2009, pp. 274-291.

Central Intelligence Agency (CIA). *The 2011 World Factbook*. 2011. Available from *www.cia.gov/library/publications/ the-world-factbook/geos/ni.html*.

Cohen, Herman J. "Africa: A Light at the End of the Tunnel?" *Air and Space Power Journal–Africa and Francophonie*, Vol. 1, No. 3, Fall 2010, pp. 6-15. Available from *www.academyofdiplomacy.org/ publications/article_archive/Africa%20by%20Cohen.pdf*.

Collier, Paul and Anke Hoeffler. *The Political Economy of Secession*. Washington DC: World Bank, Development Research Group, 2006.

Collier, Paul and Nicholas Sambanis. "Understanding Civil War: A New Agenda." *Journal of Conflict Resolution*, Vol. 46, No. 1, February 2002, pp. 3–12.

Ekanola, Adebola. "National Integration and the Survival of Nigeria in the 21st Century." *The Journal of Social, Political, and Economic Studies*, Vol. 31, Fall 2006, pp. 279-293.

Falola, Toyin. *Culture and Customs of Nigeria*. Westport, CT: Greenwood Press, 2001.

Falola, Toyin. *The History of Nigeria*. Westport, CT: Greenwood Press, 1999.

Falola, Toyin and Matthew M. Heaton. "The Works of A. E. Afigbo on Nigeria: An Historiographical Essay." *History in Africa*, Vol. 33, 2006, pp. 155-178. Available from *muse.jhu.edu/journals/hia/summary/v033/33.1falola.html*.

Hewitt, Christopher and Tom Cheetham. *Encyclopedia of Modern Separatist Movements*. Santa Barbara, CA: ABC-CLIO, 2000.

Hoffman, Adonis. "Nigeria: The Policy Conundrum." *Foreign Policy*, Vol. 101, Winter 1995, p. 146.

House Armed Services Committee. *Statement of Gen. Carter F. Ham, Commander, United States Africa Command before the House Armed Services Committee*. Washington DC: U.S. House of Representatives, April 3, 2011.

Imoh, Maurice Iroulor. *The Development of an Atlas of the Nigerian Political Evolution*. Masters Degree Thesis, Columbus, Ohio: The Ohio State University, 1977.

Institute for Security Studies Seminar Report. *South Sudan's Referendum–Geopolitical and Geostrategic Implications*. New Muckleneuk, South Africa: Institute for Security Studies, February 22, 2011.

International Crisis Group (ICG). *Lessons from Nigeria's 2011 Elections*, Africa Briefing 81. Abuja/Dakar/Brussels: International Crisis Group, September 15, 2011. Available from *www.crisisgroup.org/~/media/Files/africa/west-africa/nigeria/B81%20-%20Lessons%20from%20Nigeras%202011%20Elections.pdf.*

International Crisis Group. *Nigeria: Seizing the Moment in the Niger Delta*, Africa Briefing 60. Abuja/Dakar/Brussels: International Crisis Group, April 30, 2009. Available from *www.crisisgroup.org/~/media/Files/africa/west-africa/nigeria/B060%20Nigeria%20Seizing%20the%20Moment%20in%20the%20Niger%20Delta.pdf.*

International Crisis Group. *Nigeria: Nigeria's Faltering Federal Experiment*, Africa Report 119. Abuja/Dakar/Brussels: International Crisis Group, October 25, 2006. Available from *www.crisisgroup.org/~/media/Files/africa/west-africa/nigeria/Nigerias%20Faltering%20Federal%20Experiment.pdf.*

International Crisis Group. *Northern Nigeria: Background to Conflict*, Africa Report 168. Abuja/Dakar/Brussels: International Crisis Group, December 20, 2010. Available from *www.crisisgroup.org/~/media/Files/africa/west-africa/nigeria/168%20Northern%20Nigeria%20-%20Background%20to%20Conflict.pdf.*

Jackson, Ashley. "Nigeria: A Security Overview." *The Round Table: Commonwealth Journal of International Affairs*, Vol. 96, No. 392, October 2007, pp. 587-603.

Kenny, Joseph. "Facing Ethnicity and Religion: A Concern in Nigerian Education" in Ernest E. Uwaizie, Isaac O. Albert, and Godfrey N. Uzoigwe, eds., *Inter-Ethnic and Religious Conflict Resolution in Nigeria*. Lanham, MD: Lexington Books, 1999, pp. 49-56.

Kitson, A. E. Southern Nigeria Map. London, UK: Royal Geographical Society, 1913.

Kwaja, Chris. "Nigeria's Pernicious Drivers of Ethno-Religious Conflict." *Africa Security Brief*, No. 14, July 2011. Available from *africacenter.org/wp-content/uploads/2011/06/AfricaBrief Final_14.pdf.*

Ladan, Muhammed Tawfiq. "The Role of Youth in Inter-Ethnic and Religious Conflicts: The Kaduna/Kano Case Study" in Ernest E. Uwaizie, Isaac O. Albert, and Godfrey N. Uzoigwe, eds., *Inter-Ethnic and Religious Conflict Resolution in Nigeria*, Lanham, MD: Lexington Books, 1999, pp. 98-111.

Lake, Anthony and Christine Todd Whitman. *More Than Humanitarianism: a Strategic U.S. Approach toward Africa, Report of an Independent Task Force*. Washington DC: Council on Foreign Relations, 2006.

Lewis, Peter M. *Nigeria: Assessing Risks to Stability*. Washington DC: Center for Strategic and International Studies, June 2011. Available from *csis.org/files/publication/110623_Lewis_Nigeria_Web.pdf*.

Mimiko, Nahzeem. "Between Yugoslavia and Czechoslovakia: The Abacha Coup, the National Conference, and Prospects for Peace and Democracy in Nigeria." *Social Justice*, Vol. 22, No. 3, Fall 1995, pp. 129-142.

Morelli, Massimo and Dominic Rohner. *Natural Resource Distribution and Multiple Forms of Civil War*. New York: Columbia University, August 9, 2010. Available from *humansecuritygateway.com/documents/NaturalResourceDistributionandMultipleFormsofCivilWar.pdf*.

de Montclos, Marc-Antoine Perouse. "Conversion to Islam and Modernity in Nigeria: A View from the Underworld." *Africa Today*, Vol. 54, 2008, pp. 71-87.

The New Atlanticist Policy Blog. J. Peter Pham. "Why Nigeria Matters." The Atlantic Council, April 2011. Available from *www.acus.org/new_atlanticist/why-nigeria-matters-0*.

Newsom, Chris. *Conflict in the Niger Delta: More than a Local Affair*. Washington DC: U.S. Institute of Peace, June 2011. Available from *www.usip.org/files/resources/Conflict_Niger_Delta.pdf*.

Niger Delta Development Commission. Port Harcourt, Nigeria. Available from *www.nddc.gov.ng/masterplan.html*.

Niger Delta Working Group. *Briefing Paper on Nigeria's Niger Delta Prepared for the U.S.-Nigeria Binational Commission*, U.S.-Nigeria Binational Commission, Washington, DC, September 2010. Available from *ndwgnews.blogspot.com/p/about-ndwg.html*.

Nigerian Surveys. Southern Provinces of Nigeria Map. Lagos: Nigerian Surveys, August 1930.

Nwachuku, Levi and G. N. Uzoigwe. "Preface" in Levi Nwachuku and G. N. Uzoigwe. eds., *Troubled Journey, Nigeria since the Civil War*. Dallas, TX: University Press of America, 2004, pp. xi-xix.

Okonta, Ike. "Nigeria's Homegrown Terrorists." *Project Syndicate*, October 6, 2011. Available from *www.project-syndicate. org/commentary/okonta11/English?utm_medium=referral&utm_ source=pulsenews*.

Onoha, Freedom C. "Climate Change, Population Surge and Resource Overuse in the Lake Chad Area: Implications for Human Security in the North-East Zone of Nigeria" in Donald Anthony Mwiturubani and Jo-Ansie van Wyk, eds., *Climate Change and Natural Resources Conflicts in Africa*, Pretoria, South Africa: Institute for Security Studies, 2010, pp. 23-45. Available from *www.humansecuritygateway.com/documents/ISS_ClimateChangeand NaturalResourcesConflictsinAfica.pdf*.

Orogun, Paul S. "Resource Control, Revenue Allocation and Petroleum Politics in Nigeria: The Niger Delta Question." *GeoJournal*, Vol. 75, 2010, pp. 459-507.

Ploch, Lauren. *Africa Command: U.S. Strategic Interests and the Role of the U.S. Military in Africa*. Washington DC: Congressional Research Service, July 22, 2011.

_____. *Nigeria: Elections and Issues for Congress*. Washington DC: Congressional Research Service, January 19, 2012.

Reynolds, Jonathan T. "Nigeria and Shari'a: Religion and Politics in a West African Nation." *History Behind the Headlines*, Vol. 2, 2001, pp. 214-220.

Shelton, Dinah L., ed. "Biafra/Nigeria" in *Genocide and Crimes Against Humanity*. Seattle, WA. Available from: *eNotes.com, 2005. www.enotes.com/biafra-nigeria-reference/.*

Sodiq, Yushau. "Living in a Pluralistic World: Constraints and Opportunities." *The Muslim World*, Vol. 99, No. 4, October 2009, pp. 646-688.

Stewart, Scott. "The Rising Threat from Nigeria's Boko Haram Militant Group." *Stratfor Security Weekly*, November 10, 2011. Available from *www.stratfor.com/weekly/20111109-rising-threat-nigerias-boko-haram-militant-group?utm_source=freelist-f&utm_medium=email&utm_campaign=111110&utm_term=sweekly&utm_content=readmore&elq=a33db215cff347ffb5222bf4c45fb5d7.*

Suberu, Rotimi T. "The Supreme Court and Federalism in Nigeria." *Journal of Modern African Studies*, Vol. 46, No. 3, 2008, pp. 451–485.

Survey Department. Map of Nigeria. Lagos: Survey Department, 1953.

Topographic Section, General Staff. Lagos and Southern Nigeria map 2084. London, UK: War Office, General Staff, Topographical Section, 1905.

Transparency International. "Corruption Perceptions Index 2011." Available from *cpi.transparency.org/cpi2011/results/.*

Udo, Reuben K. *Geographical Regions of Nigeria*. Berkley, CA: University of California Press, 1970.

Umar, Muhammad Sani. "Weak States and Democratization: Ethnic and Religious Conflicts in Nigeria" in J. Craig Jenkins and Esther E. Gottlieb, eds., *Identity Conflicts: Can Violence by Regulated?* New Brunswick, NJ: Transaction Publishers, 2007.

U.S. Department of State and the Broadcasting Board of Governors Office of Inspector General. *Report of Inspection*, Report Number ISP-I-09-63. Washington, DC: The Bureau of African Affairs, August 2009. Available from *oig.state.gov/documents/organization/127270.pdf*.

U.S. Department of State. "Terrorist Designations of Boko Haram Commander Abubakar Shekau, Khalid al-Barnawi, and Abubakar Adam Kambar." Washington, DC, Media Note, Office of the Spokesperson. June 21, 2012.

United States Institute of Peace. "USIP in Nigeria." Available from *www.usip.org/node/7329/#nigeria*.

Uwazie, Queen Florence. "The Emergence of Political Terrorism in Nigeria" in Ernest E. Uwaizie, Isaac O. Albert, and G. N. Uzoigwe, eds., *Inter-Ethnic and Religious Conflict Resolution in Nigeria*. Lanham, MD: Lexington Books, 1999, pp. 113-119.

Uzoigwe, G. N. "Assessing the History of Ethnic/Religious Relations" in Ernest E. Uwaizie, Isaac O. Albert, and Godfrey N. Uzoigwe, eds., *Inter-Ethnic and Religious Conflict Resolution in Nigeria*. Lanham, MD: Lexington Books, 1999, pp. 7-18.

_____. "Nigeria to 1960: An Overview" in Levi Nwachuku and G. N. Uzoigwe, eds., *Troubled Journey, Nigeria Since the Civil War*. Dallas, TX: University Press of America, 2004, pp. 7-19.

Walter, Barbara F. "Does Conflict Beget Conflict? Explaining Recurring Civil War." *Journal of Peace Research*, Vol. 41, No. 3, May 2004, pp. 371-378.

Yakuba, J. Ademola. "Ethnicity and the Nigerian Constitutions" in Ernest E. Uwaizie, Isaac O. Albert, and G. N. Uzoigwe, eds., *Inter-Ethnic and Religious Conflict Resolution in Nigeria*. Lanham, MD: Lexington Books, 1999, pp. 37-48.

ENDNOTES

1. Anthony Lake and Christine Todd Whitman, *More Than Humanitarianism: A Strategic U.S. Approach toward Africa, Report of an Independent Task Force*, Washington DC: Council on Foreign Relations, 2006, p. 3.

2. Alexis Habiyaremye, "CHINAFRIQUE, AFRICOM, and African Natural Resources: A Modern Scramble for Africa?" *The Whitehead Journal of Diplomacy and International Relations*, Vol. 12, No. 1, Winter 2011, p. 79.

3. The Atlantic Council, J. Peter Pham, "Why Nigeria Matters," The New Atlanticist Policy Blog, April 2011, available from *www.acus.org/new_atlanticist/why-nigeria-matters-0*.

4. Lauren Ploch, *Africa Command: U.S. Strategic Interests and the Role of the U.S. Military in Africa*, Washington, DC: Congressional Research Service, July 22, 2011, pp. 14-19.

5. "Statement of Gen. Carter F. Ham, Commander, United States Africa Command before the House Armed Services Committee," Hearing before the House Armed Service Committee, April 3, 2011, Washington, DC U.S. Government Printing Office, p. 3.

6. U.S. Energy Information Administration (EIA), "Nigeria," August 2011, available from *www.eia.gov/countries/cab.cfm?fips=NI*.

7. Central Intelligence Agency (CIA), *The 2011 World Factbook*, 2011, p. Nigeria - Economy, availabale from *https://www.cia.gov/library/publications/the-world-factbook/geos/ni.html*; and Uzoigwe, "Nigeria to 1960," p. 3.

8. EIA.

9. G. N. Uzoigwe, "Nigeria to 1960: An Overview," Levi Nwachuku and G. N. Uzoigwe, eds., *Troubled Journey, Nigeria Since the Civil War*, Dallas, TX: University Press of America, 2004, p. 4.

10. The UN Mission for the Referendum in Western Sahara (MINURSO), the UN Organization Stabilization Mission in the Democratic Republic of the Congo (MONUSCO), the African Union/UN Hybrid Operation in Darfur (UNAMID), the UN Mission in Liberia (UNMIL), the UN Mission in Sudan (UNMIS), and the UN Operation in Côte d'Ivoire (UNOCI), in addition to those working as UN forces in places as distant as Haiti and Timor-Leste.

11. The United States is particularly interested in the security of the Gulf of Guinea, primarily because of its importance in exporting oil from West Africa to North America.

12. Maurice Iroulor Imoh, *The Development of an Atlas of the Nigerian Political Evolution*, Masters Degree Thesis, Columbus, Ohio: The Ohio State University, 1977, p. 85.

13. Toyin Falola, *Culture and Customs of Nigeria*, Westport, CT: Greenwood Press, 2001, p. 17; Simeon H. O. Alozieuwa, "Beyond the Ethno-Religious Theory of the Jos Conflict," *Africa Peace and Conflict Journal*, Vol. 3, No. 2, p. 26, available from *www.humansecuritygateway.com/documents/APCJ_Vol3No2Dec2010.pdf*; and Toyin Falola, *The History of Nigeria*, Westport CT: Greenwood Press, 1999, pp. 11, 68-69.

14. Ashley Jackson, "Nigeria: A Security Overview," *The Round Table: Commonwealth Journal of International Affairs*, Vol. 96, No. 392, October 2007, p. 588.

15. Isaac O. Albert, "The Sociocultural Politics of Ethnic and Religious Conflicts," Ernest E. Uwaizie, Isaac O. Albert, and Godfrey N. Uzoigwe, eds., *Inter-Ethnic and Religious Conflict Resolution in Nigeria*, Lanham, MD: Lexington Books, 1999, p. 70.

16. Falola, *Culture and Customs of Nigeria*, p. 30; International Crisis Group, *Northern Nigeria: Background to Conflict*, Africa Report 168, Abuja/Dakar/Brussels: International Crisis Group, December 20, 2010, pp. 16-20, available from *www.crisisgroup. org/~/media/Files/africa/west-africa/nigeria/168%20Northern%20 Nigeria%20-%20Background%20to%20Conflict.pdf*; and Falola, *The History of Nigeria*, p. 7.

17. Reuben K. Udo, *Geographical Regions of Nigeria*, Berkley, CA: University of California Press, 1970, p. 8; and Falola, *Culture and Customs of Nigeria*, p. 31.

18. CIA, "Nigeria - People and Society."

19. Falola, *Culture and Customs of Nigeria*, pp. 6-7; and Alozieuwa, p. 22.

20. Yushau Sodiq, "Living in a Pluralistic World: Constraints and Opportunities," *The Muslim World*, Vol. 99, No. 4, October 2009, pp. 652; and Christopher Hewitt and Tom Cheetham, *Encyclopedia of Modern Separatist Movements*, Santa Barbara, CA: ABC-CLIO, 2000, pp. 54-55.

21. ICG, *Northern Nigeria: Background to Conflict*, p. 5.

22. *Ibid.*; and Peter M. Lewis, *Nigeria: Assessing Risks to Stability*, Washington DC: Center for Strategic and International Studies, June 2011, p. 4, available from *csis.org/files/publication/110623_Lewis_Nigeria_Web.pdf*.

23. Falola, *The History of Nigeria*, p. 56; and Hewitt and Cheetham, pp. 54-55.

24. Wale Adebanwi, "The Clergy, Culture, and Political Conflicts in Nigeria," *African Studies Review*, Vol. 53, No. 3, December 2010, pp. 121-142.

25. Salisu A. Abdullahi, "Ethnicity and Ethnic Relations in Nigeria: The Case of Religious Conflict in Kano," Judy Carter, George Irani and Vamik D. Volkan, eds., *Regional and Ethnic Conflicts: Perspectives from the Front Lines*, Upper Saddle River, NJ: Pearson Prentice Hall, 2009, p. 292.

26. Abdullahi, p. 292; Falola, *The History of Nigeria*, pp. 19, 28; and ICG, *Northern Nigeria: Background to Conflict*, p. 3.

27. Roland Oliver, *The African Experience*, New York: HarperCollins Publishers, Inc., 1991, p. 157.

28. ICG, *Northern Nigeria: Background to Conflict*, p. 3.

29. Falola, *Culture and Customs of Nigeria*, p. 40; ICG, *Northern Nigeria: Background to Conflict*, p. 6; and Abdullahi, p. 293.

30. The Kala-Kato sect is also known as Maitatsine. Abdullahi, p. 293; ICG, *Northern Nigeria: Background to Conflict*, p. i and 14; Lewis, p. 11; and Conerly Casey, "Mediated Hostility, Generation, and Victimhood in Northern Nigeria," Judy Carter, George Irani and Vamik D. Volkan, eds., *Regional and Ethnic Conflicts: Perspectives from the Front Lines*, Upper Saddle River, NJ: Pearson Prentice Hall, 2009, p. 281.

31. Yushau Sodiq, "Can Muslims and Christians Live Together Peacefully in Nigeria?" *The Muslim World*, Vol. 99, No. 4, October 2009, p. 656.

32. Tony Johnson, "Boko Haram," Update: December 27, 2011, New York: Council on Foreign Relations, December 27, 2011, *www.cfr.org/africa/boko-haram/p25739*.

33. Media Note, Office of the Spokesperson, "Terrorist Designations of Boko Haram Commander Abubakar Shekau, Khalid al-Barnawi and Abubakar Adam Kambar," U.S. Department of State, Washington, DC, June 21, 2012, available from *www.state.gov/r/pa/prs/ps/2012/06/193574.htm*.

34. Scott Stewart, "The Rising Threat from Nigeria's Boko Haram Militant Group," *StratFor Security Weekly*, November 10, 2011, available from *www.stratfor.com/weekly/20111109-rising-threat-nigerias-boko-haram-militant-group?utm_source=freelist-f&utm_medium=email&utm_campaign=111110&utm_term=sweekly&utm_content=readmore&elq=a33db215cff347ffb5222bf4c45fb5d7*; and ICG, *Northern Nigeria: Background to Conflict*, p. i.

35. Jonathan T. Reynolds, "Nigeria and Shari'a: Religion and Politics in a West African Nation," *History Behind the Headlines*, Vol. 2, 2001, p. 217.

36. Falola, *Culture and Customs of Nigeria*, p. 40.

37. Reynolds, p. 217.

38. Toyin Falola and Matthew M. Heaton, "The Works of A. E. Afigbo on Nigeria: An Historiographical Essay," *History in Africa*, Vol. 33, 2006, p. 158.

39. The website *www.onlinenigeria.com/tribes* lists 371 tribes by name and location. Falola, *Culture and Customs of Nigeria*, pp. 4, 6; Alozieuwa, p. 26; ICG, *Northern Nigeria: Background to Conflict*, p. 2; and Falola, *The History of Nigeria*, pp. 5, 18.

40. The other major ethnic groups include: Kanuri, four million; Ibibo, 3.6 million; Tiv, 2.5 million; Ijaw, two million; Edo 1.7 million; Anana, Nupe, Urhollo, and Igala each around 1.2 million in 2000 in Hewitt and Cheetham, p. 206. Falola, *Culture and Customs of Nigeria*, p. 5; and Michael A. Blessing, *Nigeria's Center(s, of Gravity: A Complex and Violent Operational Environment*, Carlisle, PA: U.S. Army War College, 2008, p. 18, available from *www.dtic.mil/cgi-bin/GetTRDoc?AD=ADA478387&Location=U2&doc=GetTR Doc.pdf.*

41. Adebola Ekanola, "National Integration and the Survival of Nigeria in the 21st Century," *The Journal of Social, Political, and Economic Studies*, Vol. 31, Fall 2006, p. 280.

42. Blessing, p. 18; and Freedom C. Onoha, "Climate Change, Population Surge and Resource Overuse in the Lake Chad Area: Implications for Human Security in the North-East Zone of Nigeria," Donald Anthony Mwiturubani and Jo-Ansie van Wyk, eds., *Climate Change and Natural Resources Conflicts in Africa*, Pretoria, South Africa: Institute for Security Studies, 2010, p. 30, available from *www.humansecuritygateway.com/documents/ISS_Climate ChangeandNaturalResourcesConflictsinAfica.pdf.*

43. Abdullahi, p. 293.

44. Hewitt and Cheetham, p. 45.

45. Falola and Heaton, p. 158.

46. Falola and Heaton, pp. 158-159.

47. G. N. Uzoigwe, "Assessing the History of Ethnic/Religious Relations," Ernest E. Uwaizie, Isaac O. Albert, and Godfrey N. Uzoigwe, eds., *Inter-Ethnic and Religious Conflict Resolution in Nigeria*, Lanham, MD: Lexington Books, 1999, p. 15; and Falola and Heaton, p. 157.

48. Uzoigwe, "Assessing the History of Ethnic/Religious Relations," p. 7.

49. Udo, p. 1; and CIA, "People and Society," and "Government."

50. Falola, *The History of Nigeria*, pp. 77, 83.

51. Hewitt and Cheetham, p. 206.

52. Ekanola, p. 287.

53. Matthew Todd Bradley, "Inter-Ethnic Antagonism in Post-Colonial Nigeria: Ethnicity vs. Symbolic Nationalism," *Journal of Cultural Studies*, Vol. 7, No. 1, 2006, p. 71.

54. Abdullahi, p. 292; Falola and Heaton, p. 169; and Uzoigwe, "Nigeria to 1960," pp. 10-11. The non-centralized societies include Igbo, Ibibio, Ijo, Tiv, Idoma, Angass, Yako, Mbembe, and Ekoi.

55. Falola and Heaton, pp. 157-159.

56. Falola, *Culture and Customs of Nigeria*, p. 17.

57. Uzoigwe, "Nigeria to 1960," p. 13. Uzoigwe believes that the British imposed the north-south factionalism on Nigeria then, when none existed before in Nigerian history.

58. Falola and Heaton, p. 161.

59. Falola, *The History of Nigeria*, p. 70.

60. *Ibid.*, p. 73.

61. Falola, *Culture and Customs of Nigeria*, p. 17.

62. Falola and Heaton, p. 161; Falola, *The History of Nigeria*, pp. 72, 74; and Falola, *Culture and Customs of Nigeria*, p. 17.

63. Adekeye Adebajo, *The Curse of Berlin: Africa After the Cold War*, New York: Columbia University Press, 2010, p. xiii.

64. ICG, *Northern Nigeria: Background to Conflict*, p. 2; Uzoigwe, "Assessing the History of Ethnic/Religious Relations," p. 8; and Falola, *The History of Nigeria*, p. 11.

65. J. Ademola Yakuba, "Ethnicity and the Nigerian Constitutions," Ernest E. Uwaizie, Isaac O. Albert, and Godfrey N. Uzoigwe, eds., *Inter-Ethnic and Religious Conflict Resolution in Nigeria*, Lanham, MD: Lexington Books, 1999, p. 39; and Falola, *The History of Nigeria*, pp. 92, 109.

66. Falola, *The History of Nigeria*, p. 104.

67. Casey, p. 279; and Falola, *The History of Nigeria*, pp. 116-118.

68. Six states from the north, three from the secessionist east, and conversion of Western and Midwestern Regions and Lagos Federal Territory to states.

69. Falola, *The History of Nigeria*, pp. 122, 129.

70. Lewis, pp. 5-6; and Yakuba, p. 39.

71. Falola, *The History of Nigeria*, pp. 227-228.

72. ICG, *Northern Nigeria: Background to Conflict*, p. 8; Uzoigwe, "Assessing the History of Ethnic/Religious Relations," p. 16; and Falola, *The History of Nigeria*, p. 11.

73. Yakuba, p. 39.

74. Falola, *The History of Nigeria*, p. 226; and ICG, *Nigeria: Nigeria's Faltering Federal Experiment*, Africa Report 119, Abuja/Dakar/Brussels: International Crisis Group, October 25, 2006, p. 2, available from *www.crisisgroup.org/~/media/Files/africa/west-africa/nigeria/Nigerias%20Faltering%20Federal%20Experiment.pdf*.

75. Northeast, northwest, north-central, southeast, southwest, and south-south geopolitical zones.

76. Abdullahi, p. 292; and Falola, *The History of Nigeria*, p. 202.

77. Yakuba, p. 40.

78. Lewis, p. 8.

79. Uzoigwe, "Nigeria to 1960: An Overview," pp. 5, 7.

80. CIA, Nigeria-Geography; and Falola, *Culture and Customs of Nigeria*, p. 9.

81. Udo, p. 2.

82. Uzoigwe, "Nigeria to 1960: An Overview," p. 3.

83. Falola, *Culture and Customs of Nigeria*, p. 3; and Falola, *The History of Nigeria*, p. 2.

84. Falola, *The History of Nigeria*, p. 2; and Udo, p. 3.

85. Falola, *Culture and Customs of Nigeria*, p. 3.

86. *Ibid.*, pp. 2-3; and Udo, pp. 8-9.

87. CIA, "Nigeria - Geography," "United States - Geography," "United Kingdom - Geography."

88. CIA, "Nigeria - Economy."

89. Udo, p. 6.

90. Blessing, p. 16.

91. Falola, *Culture and Customs of Nigeria*, p. 12; Lewis, p. 5; and Udo p. 3.

92. Falola, *The History of Nigeria*, pp. 143-144; Onoha p. 25-26; Falola, *Culture and Customs of Nigeria*, p. 12; and Adebajo, p. 124.

93. Uzoigwe, "Nigeria to 1960: An Overview," p. 3.

94. Falola, *The History of Nigeria*, pp. 2-3; and Onoha, pp. 25-26.

95. Blessing, p. 16.

96. Onoha, pp. 24-28.

97. Udo, p. 4; Falola, *The History of Nigeria*, p. 199; and CIA, "Nigeria - Geography."

98. Mark Moritz, "Understanding Herder-Farmer Conflicts in West Africa: Outline of a Processual Approach," *Human Organization*, Vol. 69, No. 2, Summer 2010, p. 138.

99. CIA, "Nigeria - People and Society."

100. Falola, *The History of Nigeria*, p. 4.

101. CIA, "Nigeria - People and Society."

102. Udo, p. 5; and Falola, *Culture and Customs of Nigeria*, p. 8.

103. Falola, *Culture and Customs of Nigeria*, pp. 2-3.

104. ICG, *Northern Nigeria: Background to Conflict*, p. 22.

105. ICG, *Nigeria: Nigeria's Faltering Federal Experiment*, pp. 12-13.

106. Falola, *The History of Nigeria*, p. 33.

107. Albert, p. 72.

108. Hewitt and Cheetham, p. 45.

109. CIA, "Nigeria - People and Society."

110. ICG, *Northern Nigeria: Background to Conflict*, p. 22; and Falola, *The History of Nigeria*, p. 33.

111. CIA, "Nigeria - People and Society."

112. Falola, *The History of Nigeria*, pp. 42-43.

113. *Ibid.*, p. 78.

114. *Ibid.*, p. 10.

115. Scott Stewart, "The Rising Threat from Nigeria's Boko Haram Militant Group;" and ICG, *Northern Nigeria: Background to Conflict*, p. i.

116. Hewitt and Cheetham, p. 45.

117. ICG, *Northern Nigeria: Background to Conflict*, p. 10.

118. *Ibid.*, p. 10.

119. Falola, *The History of Nigeria*, p. 77.

120. Yushau Sodiq, "Can Muslims and Christians Live Together Peacefully in Nigeria?" *The Muslim World*, Vol. 99, No. 4, October 2009, p. 650.

121. Ekanola, p. 286.

122. Ogechi Anyanwu, "The Anglo-American-Nigerian Collaboration in Nigeria's Higher Education Reform: The Cold War and Decolonization, 1948-1960," *Journal of Colonialism & Colonial History*, Vol. 3, Winter 2010, pp. 183-202.

123. Falola, *The History of Nigeria*, p. 27; and Falola, *Culture and Customs of Nigeria*, p. 11.

124. Udo, p. 7.

125. ICG, *Northern Nigeria: Background to Conflict*, p. 5; and Falola, *Culture and Customs of Nigeria*, p. 12.

126. Fidelis Allen and Ufo Okeke-Uzodike, "Oil, Politics, and Conflict in the Niger Delta: A Nonkilling Analysis," *Africa Peace and Conflict Journal*, Vol. 3, No. 2, p. 32, available from *www.humansecuritygateway.com/documents/APCJ_Vol3No2Dec2010.pdf*.

127. Falola, *The History of Nigeria*, p. 138.

128. *Ibid.*, pp. 112, 132.

129. Nahzeem Mimiko, "Between Yugoslavia and Czechoslovakia: The Abacha Coup, the National Conference, and Prospects for Peace and Democracy in Nigeria," *Social Justice*, Vol. 22, Fall 1995, p. 129.

130. Allen and Okeke-Uzodike, p. 33; and Bonnie Ayodele, "Silence on Climate Change and Natural Resources Conflict in Nigeria: The Niger Delta Region Experience," Donald Anthony Mwiturubani and Jo-Ansie van Wyk, eds., *Climate Change and Natural Resources Conflicts in Africa*, Pretoria, South Africa: Institute for Security Studies, 2010, p. 111.

131. Falola and Heaton, pp. 170-171.

132. Imoh, p. 57.

133. Udo, p. 8.

134. Falola, *Culture and Customs of Nigeria*, p. 9; and CIA, "Nigeria - Economy."

135. Stewart.

136. Adebajo, p. 125.

137. Lewis, p. 7; and CIA, "Nigeria - Economy."

138. The use of Gross Domestic Product (GDP) Purchasing Power Parity (PPP) is a relatively new method of measuring a country's economic production, rather than the previous method of calculating GDP based upon an official exchange rate. PPP measurements reduce the error that transitory U.S. dollar, the usual medium used to ensure like comparisons, exchange rate

spikes induce, and accounts for the difficulty in obtaining common basic necessities for living. Using the GDP PPP usually increases the amount of economic production per person in lesser-developed countries, thereby reducing the perception of poverty suffered when compared to unadjusted figures. Since this comparison starts with figures computed with the official exchange rate at the time, a GDP per capita of $1,470 based on the 2010 official exchange rate is also used. The bottom line is that the average share of a Nigerians' slice of the country's economic pie has remained stagnant over 40 years and dipped considerably in the interim, despite Nigeria's enormous natural resource wealth. The GDP PPP in Nigeria for 2010 is $2,500, ranking it 175th lowest in the world. These comparisons are based on data from the CIA *2010 World Factbook*, "Nigeria - Economy"; and Falola, *The History of Nigeria*, p. 16.

139. Hewitt and Cheetham, p. 206.

140. Lewis, pp. 9-10, 12-13.

141. Transparency International, "Corruption Perceptions Index 2011," available from *cpi.transparency.org/cpi2011/results/*.

142. Blessing, p. 17.

143. Falola, *Culture and Customs of Nigeria*, pp. 12-13.

144. Ike Okonta, "Nigeria's Homegrown Terrorists," Project Syndicate, October 6, 2011, available from *www.project-syndicate.org/commentary/okonta11/English?utm_medium=referral&utm_source=pulsenews*.

145. Daniel Agbiboa, "The Corruption-Underdevelopment Nexus in Africa: Which Way Nigeria?!" *The Journal of Social, Political, and Economic Studies*, Vol. 35, No. 4, Winter 2010, p. 474.

146. Abdullahi, p. 298; and Falola, *The History of Nigeria*, p. 14.

147. Herman J. Cohen, "Africa: A Light at the End of the Tunnel?" *Air and Space Power Journal–Africa and Francophonie*, Vol. 1, No. 3, Fall 2010, pp. 11-12, available from *www.academyof diplomacy.org/publications/article_archive/Africa%20by%20Cohen.pdf*.

148. Okonta.

149. Falola, *The History of Nigeria*, pp. 36, 152, 209.

150. Casey, p. 276.

151. Falola, *The History of Nigeria*, p. 198.

152. Paul S. Orogun, "Resource Control, Revenue Allocation and Petroleum Politics in Nigeria: The Niger Delta Question," *GeoJournal*, Vol. 75, 2010, p. 459.

153. Falola, *The History of Nigeria*, p. 199.

154. Allen and Okeke-Uzodike, p. 33.

155. *Ibid.*, p. 39; and Ayodele, p. 114.

156. Akpomuvie Orhioghene Benedict, "Breaking Barriers to Transformation of the Niger Delta Region of Nigeria: A Human Development Paradigm," *Journal of Sustainable Development*, Vol. 4, No. 3, June 2011, p. 211.

157. Judith Burdin Asuni, *Special Report: Blood Oil in the Niger Delta*, Washington, DC: United States Institute of Peace, August 2009, p. 6.

158. Annegret Mahler, *Nigeria: A Prime Example of the Resource Curse? Revisiting the Oil-Violence Link in the Niger Delta*, Hamburg, Germany: German Institute of Global and Area Studies, January 2010, p. 13.

159. Paul Collier and Anke Hoeffler, *The Political Economy of Secession*, Washington DC: World Bank, Development Research Group, 2006, pp. 217-219.

160. Falola, *The History of Nigeria*, p. 230; and Lewis, p. 6.

161. Lewis, pp. 2, 7.

162. Alozieuwa, p. 23.

163. *Ibid.*, pp. 29-30.

164. Chris Kwaja, "Nigeria's Pernicious Drivers of Ethno-Religious Conflict," *Africa Security Brief*, No. 14, July 2011, p. 4, available from *africacenter.org/wp-content/uploads/2011/06/AfricaBrief Final_14.pdf*; Chris Newsom, *Conflict in the Niger Delta: More than a Local Affair*, Washington DC: United States Institute of Peace, June 2011, p. 3, available from *www.usip.org/files/resources/Conflict_ Niger_Delta.pdf*; and Falola, *The History of Nigeria*, p. 91.

165. Alozieuwa, pp. 25, 29-30; ICG, *Nigeria: Nigeria's Faltering Federal Experiment*, p. 13.

166. *Ibid.*, p. 25; and Kwaja, p. 4.

167. Hewitt and Cheetham, p. 206.

168. Adebajo, pp. 1-2.

169. Lewis, p. 9.

170. Alozieuwa, p. 26; Kwaja, pp. 1-2.

171. ICG, *Nigeria: Nigeria's Faltering Federal Experiment*, pp. 3-4, 12.

172. Newsom, p. 5; and Falola, *Culture and Customs of Nigeria*, p. 25.

173. Casey, p. 285; and Uwazie, pp. 116-117.

174. Albert, pp. 70, 77; and Kwaja, p. 1.

175. Falola, *The History of Nigeria*, pp. 107-108 Abdullahi, p. 295; Kwaja, p. 3; and Muhammad Sani Umar, "Weak States and Democratization: Ethnic and Religious Conflicts in Nigeria," J. Craig Jenkins and Esther E. Gottlieb, eds., *Identity Conflicts: Can Violence by Regulated?* New Brunswick, NJ: Transaction Publishers, 2007, p. 265.

176. Lewis, pp. 1, 8; Newsom, p. 7; and Abdullahi, p. 295.

177. *Ibid.*, p. 5; and Albert, p. 81.

178. Falola, *The History of Nigeria*, p. 91; Kwaja, p. 2; and Alozieuwa, pp. 29-30.

179. ICG, *Nigeria: Nigeria's Faltering Federal Experiment*, p. 9; and International Crisis Group, *Lessons from Nigeria's 2011 Elections*, Africa Briefing 81, Abuja/Dakar/Brussels: International Crisis Group, September 15, 2011, p. 8, available from *www. crisisgroup.org/~/media/Files/africa/west-africa/nigeria/B81%20-%20 Lessons%20from%20Nigeras%202011%20Elections.pdf*.

180. Falola, *The History of Nigeria*, pp. 130, 155; and ICG, *Nigeria: Nigeria's Faltering Federal Experiment*, p. 5.

181. Falola, *Culture and Customs of Nigeria*, p. 21; and Casey, p. 276.

182. ICG, *Nigeria: Nigeria's Faltering Federal Experiment*, pp. 5-6; Lewis, pp. 10-12.

183. Abdullahali, p. 296.

184. Alozieuwa, p. 27; Falola, *The History of Nigeria*, pp. 103, 170.

185. Falola, *The History of Nigeria*, p. 153; and Falola, *Culture and Customs of Nigeria*, p. 13.

186. Falola, *Culture and Customs of Nigeria*, pp. 22-24; and Falola, *The History of Nigeria*, pp. 164, 176-179.

187. Alozieuwa, pp. 24, 27; Abdullahi, p. 297.

188. ICG, *Nigeria: Nigeria's Faltering Federal Experiment*, p. 9.

189. Falola, *The History of Nigeria*, p. 171.

190. Uwazie, pp. 116-117.

191. Falola and Heaton, pp. 170-171.

192. Lewis, p. 7; and ICG, *Lessons from Nigeria's 2011 Elections*, p. 11.

193. Umar, p. 269.

194. Okonta; and Uzoigwe, "Assessing the History of Ethnic/ Religious Relations," p. 16.

195. Adebajo, p. 328.

196. Paul Collier and Nicholas Sambanis, "Understanding Civil War: A New Agenda," *Journal of Conflict Resolution*, Vol. 46, No. 1, February 2002, p. 5.

197. "Timeline-Ethnic and Religious Unrest in Nigeria," *Reuters*, January 24, 2012, available from *www.trust.org/alert-net/news/timeline-ethnic-and-religious-unrest-in-nigeria/*; and ICG, *Nigeria: Nigeria's Faltering Federal Experiment*, pp. 12-13.

198. "South Sudan's Referendum-Geopolitical and Geostra-tegic Implications," *ISS Seminar Report*, New Muckleneuk, South Africa: Institute for Security Studies, February 22, 2011, p. 1.

199. Imoh, pp. 53-54, 57.

200. Topographic Section, General Staff, Lagos and South-ern Nigeria, Map 2084, London, UK: War Office, General Staff, Topographic Section, 1905. Modern southern Nigeria is defined by the northern borders of Cross River, Enugu, Anambra, Delta, Edo, Ondo, Osun, and Oyo states, and also contained what would become Akwa Ibom, Abia, Imo, Rivers, Ogun, and Lagos states. Samuel Aryeetey Atoh, "Africa South of the Sahara," Douglas S. Johnson, Viola Haarmann, Merrill L. Johnson, and David L. Clawson, eds., *World Regional Geography*, Upper Saddle Brook, NJ: Pearson Prentice Hall, 2010, p. 438.

201. A. E. Kitson, Southern Nigeria Map, London, UK: Royal Geographical Society, 1913; Nigerian Surveys, Southern Provinces of Nigeria Map, Lagos: Nigerian Surveys, August 1930; and Survey Department, Map of Nigeria, Lagos: Survey Department, 1953.

202. Imoh, pp. 53-58; Topographic Section, General Staff, 1905.

203. *Ibid.*, p. 80.

204. *Ibid.*, pp. 49-50.

205. *Ibid.*, p. 47.

206. Hewitt and Cheetham, p. 45; and American School of International Service, "The Biafran War," Washington DC: American University School of International Service, November 1997, available from *www1.american.edu/ted/ice/biafra.htm*.

207. Paul Collier and Anke Hoeffler, *The Political Economy of Secession*, pp. 4-9.

208. *Ibid.*, p. 17.

209. Benedict, p. 211.

210. ICG, *Nigeria: Nigeria's Faltering Federal Experiment*, pp. 8, 16; Blessing, pp. 7-9; and Collier and Hoeffler, *The Political Economy of Secession*, p. 18.

211. Including the modern states of Kwara, Kogi, Benue, Plateau, Taraba, Niger, and southern two-thirds of Adamawan states. Imoh, pp. 47-53; and Atoh p. 438.

212. Uzoigwe, "Nigeria to 1960," p. 8; and Imoh, pp. 49-50.

213. "Biafra/Nigeria," Dinah L. Shelton, ed., *Genocide and Crimes Against Humanity*, Vol. 1, 2005, Seattle, WA, available from *eNotes.com. www.enotes.com/biafra-nigeria-reference/*.

214. Matthew Todd Bradley, "Inter-Ethnic Antagonism in Post-Colonial Nigeria: Ethnicity vs. Symbolic Nationalism," *Journal of Cultural Studies*, Vol. 7, No. 1, 2006, p. 71.

215. Barbara F. Walter, "Does Conflict Beget Conflict? Explaining Recurring Civil War," *Journal of Peace Research*, Vol. 41, No. 3, May 2004, p. 372.

216. CIA, "Nigeria - Economy."

217. Rotimi T. Suberu, "The Supreme Court and Federalism in Nigeria," *Journal of Modern African Studies*, Vol. 46, No. 3, 2008, pp. 451–485.

218. Lewis, p. 14.

219. Levi Nwachuku and G. N. Uzoigwe, "Preface," Levi Nwachuku and G. N. Uzoigwe, eds., *Troubled Journey, Nigeria Since the Civil War*, Dallas, TX: University Press of America, 2004, p. xix.

220. Adonis Hoffman, "Nigeria: The Policy Conundrum," *Foreign Policy*, Vol. 101, Winter 1995, p. 146.

221. Lauren Ploch, *Nigeria: Elections and Issues for Congress*, Washington DC: Congressional Research Service, January 19, 2012, p. 17.

222. Ploch, *Africa Command*, p. 1.

223. *Nigeria Country Report* May 2012, The Economist Intelligence Unit Limited, 2012, pp. 4-5, 11-12.

224. Niger Delta Working Group, Briefing Paper on Nigeria's Niger Delta Prepared for the U.S.-Nigeria Binational Commission, Washington, DC, September 2010, available from *ndwgnews.blogspot.com/p/about-ndwg.html*.

225. Niger Delta Development Commission, available from *www.nddc.gov.ng/masterplan.html*.

226. Blessing, pp. 20-21.

227. ICG, *Lessons from Nigeria's 2011 Elections*, p. 14.

228. "West Africa: Regional Piracy Response Will Take Time," OxResearch Daily Brief Service, October 19, 2011, available from *relooney.fatcow.com/SI_FAO-Africa-2012/Oxford-Piracy_2.pdf*.

229. Asuni, pp. 14, 16.

230. United States Institute of Peace, "USIP in Nigeria," available from *www.usip.org/node/7329/#nigeria.*

www.ingramcontent.com/pod-product-compliance
Lightning Source LLC
Chambersburg PA
CBHW060154290526
45789CB00003B/1037